Econometric Models of
U.S. Energy Demand

Econometric Models of U.S. Energy Demand

Robert Halvorsen
University of Washington

Lexington Books
D.C. Heath and Company
Lexington, Massachusetts
Toronto

Library of Congress Cataloging in Publication Data

Halvorsen, Robert.
  Econometric models of U.S. energy demand.

  Bibliography: p.
  Includes index.
  1. Electric utilities—United States—Mathematical models. 2. Energy
policy—United States—Mathematical models. I. Title.
HD9685.U5H34   338.4'7'621   77-81791
ISBN 0-669-01942-9

Published simultaneously in Canada.

Printed in the United States of America.

International Standard Book Number: 0-669-01942-9

Library of Congress Catalog Card Number: 77-81791

To my parents

Contents

	List of Tables	xi
	Preface	xiii
Chapter 1	**Introduction and Summary**	1
Part I	*Long-Run Demand for Electricity*	5
Chapter 2	**Structure of the Electricity Demand Models**	7
	Introduction	7
	The Dependence of Price on Quantity	7
	Estimation Procedures	9
	Long-Run and Short-Run Elasticities	12
	Dynamic Cross-Section Models	13
	Summary	15
Chapter 3	**Residential Electricity Demand Equation**	19
	Introduction	19
	Specification of the Demand Equation	19
	Empirical Results: Static Model	24
	Empirical Results: Dynamic Models	29
	Empirical Results: Disaggregated Samples	32
	Concluding Comments	34
Chapter 4	**Residential Electricity Price and Reduced-Form Equations**	37
	Introduction	37
	Specification of the Price Equation	37
	Empirical Results: Price Equation	40
	Derivation of the Reduced-Form Equation	45
	Direct Estimation of the Reduced-Form Equation	47
	Total Elasticities of Demand and Expenditure	48
Chapter 5	**Commercial and Industrial Electricity Demand**	55
	Introduction	55
	Specification of Electricity Price Equations	55
	Specification of Commercial Electricity Demand Equation	56

viii

Specification of Industrial Electricity Demand
    Equation   59
Data Sources   60
Empirical Results: Commercial Sector   60
Empirical Results: Industrial Sector   62

Part II   Substitution among Types of Energy   67

Chapter 6   Derivation of Energy Demand Models Using Duality
               Theory   69

Introduction   69
Interfuel Substitution in Electric Power Generation   69
Energy Substitution in Manufacturing   76
Concluding Comments   82

Chapter 7   Interfuel Substitution in Electric Power Generation   85

Introduction   85
Estimation Procedures   86
Performance of the Model   88
Elasticity Estimates   90
Tests of Hypotheses   93
Concluding Comments   94

Chapter 8   Energy Substitution in Manufacturing   99

Introduction   99
Estimation Procedures   100
Performance of the Model   101
Parameter Estimates   104
Elasticity Estimates   105
Tests of Hypotheses   121
Concluding Comments   123

Part III   Dynamic Models of Energy Demand   133

Chapter 9   Short-Run Elasticities of Demand for Residential
               Electricity   135

Introduction   135
The Model   135
Estimation Procedures   139
Elasticity Estimates   141

Econometric Models of
U.S. Energy Demand

Econometric Models of U.S. Energy Demand

Robert Halvorsen
University of Washington

Lexington Books
D.C. Heath and Company
Lexington, Massachusetts
Toronto

Library of Congress Cataloging in Publication Data

Halvorsen, Robert.
    Econometric models of U.S. energy demand.

    Bibliography: p.
    Includes index.
    1. Electric utilities—United States—Mathematical models. 2. Energy policy—United States—Mathematical models. I. Title.
HD9685.U5H34   338.4'7'621   77–81791
ISBN 0-669-01942-9

Published simultaneously in Canada.

Printed in the United States of America.

International Standard Book Number: 0-669-01942-9

Library of Congress Catalog Card Number: 77-81791

To my parents

Contents

List of Tables   xi

Preface   xiii

Chapter 1   **Introduction and Summary**   1

Part I   *Long-Run Demand for Electricity*   5

Chapter 2   **Structure of the Electricity Demand Models**   7

Introduction   7
The Dependence of Price on Quantity   7
Estimation Procedures   9
Long-Run and Short-Run Elasticities   12
Dynamic Cross-Section Models   13
Summary   15

Chapter 3   **Residential Electricity Demand Equation**   19

Introduction   19
Specification of the Demand Equation   19
Empirical Results: Static Model   24
Empirical Results: Dynamic Models   29
Empirical Results: Disaggregated Samples   32
Concluding Comments   34

Chapter 4   **Residential Electricity Price and Reduced-Form Equations**   37

Introduction   37
Specification of the Price Equation   37
Empirical Results: Price Equation   40
Derivation of the Reduced-Form Equation   45
Direct Estimation of the Reduced-Form Equation   47
Total Elasticities of Demand and Expenditure   48

Chapter 5   **Commercial and Industrial Electricity Demand**   55

Introduction   55
Specification of Electricity Price Equations   55
Specification of Commercial Electricity Demand
     Equation   56

Specification of Industrial Electricity Demand
    Equation   59
Data Sources   60
Empirical Results: Commercial Sector   60
Empirical Results: Industrial Sector   62

Part II   *Substitution among Types of Energy*   67

Chapter 6   **Derivation of Energy Demand Models Using Duality Theory**   69

Introduction   69
Interfuel Substitution in Electric Power Generation   69
Energy Substitution in Manufacturing   76
Concluding Comments   82

Chapter 7   **Interfuel Substitution in Electric Power Generation**   85

Introduction   85
Estimation Procedures   86
Performance of the Model   88
Elasticity Estimates   90
Tests of Hypotheses   93
Concluding Comments   94

Chapter 8   **Energy Substitution in Manufacturing**   99

Introduction   99
Estimation Procedures   100
Performance of the Model   101
Parameter Estimates   104
Elasticity Estimates   105
Tests of Hypotheses   121
Concluding Comments   123

Part III   *Dynamic Models of Energy Demand*   133

Chapter 9   **Short-Run Elasticities of Demand for Residential Electricity**   135

Introduction   135
The Model   135
Estimation Procedures   139
Elasticity Estimates   141

Tests of Dynamic Specification   142
Concluding Comments   148

Chapter 10   **A Dynamic Model of Aggregate Energy Demand in
                 Manufacturing**   151

Introduction   151
The Model   151
Empirical Results   155
Concluding Comments   159

References   161

Index   167

About the Author   173

List of Tables

3–1	Specification of the Residential Demand Equation	20
3–2	Estimates of Parameters of the Residential Demand Equation: Pooled Sample	25
3–3	Beta Coefficients for the Residential Demand Equation	27
3–4	Estimates of Parameters of the Residential Demand Equation: Individual Cross-Sections	28
3–5	Residential Demand Equation with Lagged Explanatory Variables	30
3–6	Residential Demand Equation with Distributed Lags	31
3–7	Residential Demand Equation: Disaggregation by Geographic Area	33
3–8	Residential Demand Equation: Disaggregation by Value of Electricity Price	34
4–1	Specification of the Residential Price Equation	38
4–2	Estimates of Parameters of the Residential Price Equation: Pooled Sample	40
4–3	Beta Coefficients for the Residential Price Equation	41
4–4	Estimates of Parameters of the Residential Price Equation: Individual Cross-Sections	42
4–5	Residential Price Equation with Lagged Explanatory Variables	43
4–6	Residential Price Equation with Distributed Lags	44
4–7	Residential Price Equation: Disaggregation by Geographic Area	46
4–8	Estimates of Parameters of the Residential Reduced-Form Equation: Pooled Sample	48
4A–1	Specification of the Residential Reduced-Form Equation: City Data	52
4A–2	Estimates of Parameters of the Residential Reduced-Form Equation: City Data	54
5–1	Specification of the Commercial and Industrial Price Equations	56
5–2	Specification of the Commercial and Industrial Demand Equations	57
5–3	Estimates of Parameters of the Commercial Demand Equations	61
5–4	Estimates of Parameters of the Price Equations Incorporating Cost Variables	63
5–5	Estimates of Parameters of the Price Equations Incorporating TEB Variables	64

xii

5-6	Estimates of Parameters of the Industrial Demand Equations	65
7-1	Estimates of Parameters of the Normalized Restricted Profit Function	89
7-2	Estimates of Price Elasticities: Coal-Gas Sample	90
7-3	Estimates of Price Elasticities: Coal-Oil Sample	91
7-4	Estimates of Price Elasticities: Oil-Gas Sample	92
7-5	Estimates of Cross-Elasticities of Substitution: Electric Power Generation	94
7-6	Elasticities of Demand and Substitution at Means of Data: Electric Power Generation	95
7-7	Tests of Hypotheses: Electric Power Generation	96
8-1	Energy Consumption by Two-Digit Industries, 1974	101
8-2	Tests of Cross-Equation Equality Restrictions: Manufacturing	102
8-3	Signs of Principal Minors: Manufacturing	103
8-4	Estimates of Parameters of the Cost Function: 1971	106
8-5	Estimates of Parameters of the Cost Function: 1962	108
8-6	Estimates of Parameters of the Cost Function: 1958	110
8-7	Estimates of Price Elasticities: Manufacturing, 1971	112
8-8	Estimates of Price Elasticities: Manufacturing, 1962	114
8-9	Estimates of Price Elasticities: Manufacturing, 1958	116
8-10	Estimates of Allen Cross-Elasticities of Substitution: Manufacturing, 1971	119
8-11	Estimates of Aggregate Manufacturing Price Elasticities: Total Energy Input Constant	120
8-12	Estimates of Aggregate Manufacturing Price Elasticities: Total Energy Input Variable	121
8-13	Tests for Structural Change in Technology: Manufacturing	122
8-14	Tests of Cobb-Douglas Functional Form: Manufacturing	123
8A-1	Parameter Estimates: Other Industries, 1971	128
8A-2	Estimates of Price Elasticities: Other Industries, 1971	130
9-1	Estimates of Short-Run Elasticities: Model Incorporating Equation 9.16	143
9-2	Estimates of Short-Run Elasticities: Model Incorporating Equation 9.17	145
9-3	Tests of the Dynamic Specification of the Demand Equation	148
10-1	Long-Run Equilibrium Demand Equations: Manufacturing	153
10-2	Estimates of Parameters of the Dynamic Model: Manufacturing	157
10-3	Adjustment Coefficients: Manufacturing	158
10-4	Time Path of Energy Price Elasticities: Manufacturing	159

Preface

The research reported in this book was performed over a period of six years. The major topics considered, listed in chronological order, are residential demand for electricity, commercial and industrial demand for electricity, interfuel substitution in electric power generation, energy substitution in manufacturing, and dynamic energy demand in manufacturing.

The most recent data available at the time of the original research on residential electricity demand were for 1969. The short-run residential demand models have been reestimated with data through 1975. The long-run models have not been reestimated because the increasingly unsettled condition of energy markets since 1969 would prevent the interpretation of cross-sectional results as long-run elasticities.

For the most part, differences across chapters in econometric methods used are due to differences in the issues addressed, rather than to differences in the time at which the research was performed. An exception is that some differences between the procedures used in Chapters 7 and 8 reflect the very rapid development of research methods based on duality theory during the period. Specifically, the procedures used in Chapter 8 to calculate standard errors of elasticities at the means of the data, and to measure goodness of fit, are superior to those used in Chapter 7.

Chapters 2, 3, 4, and part of 9 are based on my doctoral research (Halvorsen 1972). Some of the results were reported in a paper in the *Review of Economics and Statistics* (Halvorsen 1975). I am grateful for permission to use this material here. The research was supported by a National Science Foundation grant to the Environmental Systems Program at Harvard University. I am indebted to Martin Feldstein and Henry Jacoby for stimulating my interest in this topic and for helpful comments on my research.

Chapter 5 is taken from a paper published in the *Southern Economic Journal* (Halvorsen 1976). Their permission to use the material here is appreciated. Research for the paper was supported by the Faculty Research Fund of the University of Washington.

The research on interfuel substitution in electric power generation reported in Chapters 6 and 7 was performed jointly with Scott E. Atkinson and appeared in the *Journal of Political Economy* (Atkinson and Halvorsen 1976a). I am grateful to my coauthor and the University of Chicago Press for permission to use this material. Our research was supported by the Office of Energy Systems, Federal Energy Administration. Views expressed are our own and do not represent in any way policies of the Federal Energy Administration. The paper benefitted from comments by Ernst R. Berndt, Lawrence J. Lau, and David Nissen.

The research on industrial demand for energy that is reported in Chapters 6, 8, and 10 was supported by a grant to the National Bureau of Economic Research from the National Science Foundation RANN Program. The chapters are not official NBER publications because they have not been reviewed by the board of directors.

I appreciate the helpful comments of Ernst R. Berndt, Melvyn Fuss, Sherman Maisel, and Mark Rodekohr on the material in Chapters 6 and 8 and of Elie Appelbaum and James Edmonds on the material in Chapter 10. Highly competent research assistance was provided by Jay Ford, Jean Baker, and John Wills. Some of the results in Chapter 8 were reported in an article in the *Review of Economics and Statistics* (Halvorsen 1977), and permission to use this material here is appreciated.

The entire manuscript was typed by Marian Bolan. Her skill and patience greatly facilitated the completion of this book.

Econometric Models of
U.S. Energy Demand

1 Introduction and Summary

Discussions of proposed public policies toward energy have frequently involved profound disagreements concerning the determinants of energy demand. The estimation of econometric models of energy demand offers a promising approach for improving the quality of information available for analysis of public energy policies. This book presents the results of research on econometric models of demand for several major energy markets.

Part I discusses long-run models of electricity demand in the residential, commercial, and industrial sectors. The general structure of the models is described in Chapter 2. The use of declining block rates for electricity makes electricity price a function of the quantity purchased. The issues this raises for the demand model include the choice of electricity price variable, identification of the demand equation, and the distinction between direct and total elasticities of demand.

Economic theory indicates that marginal price is the most appropriate variable to include in the demand equation, but the available data are for average rather than marginal price. It is shown in Chapter 2 that for the log-linear equations used here, the estimates of the elasticities are not affected by the use of data on average rather than marginal price.

Identification of the demand equation is achieved by including a price equation in the model. Estimates of direct elasticities of demand are obtained from the structural demand equation. Estimates of total elasticities of demand are obtained from the reduced-form equation for quantity purchased. The reduced-form equation is both derived from the estimated structural equations and estimated directly using typical electric bill (TEB) data (U.S. Federal Power Commission, various).

Estimation results for the residential demand equation are discussed in Chapter 3. The estimated long-run elasticity of demand with respect to electricity price is −1.15. The estimated income elasticity is 0.51, and the estimated elasticity with respect to gas price is 0.04. Disaggregation of the sample by geographic area indicates that there are significant differences in the characteristics of demand across regions. Disaggregation by the value of electricity price provides little support for the hypothesis that the own-price elasticity of demand is a function of the level of electricity price.

Estimation results for the residential electricity price equation are presented in Chapter 4. Quantity purchased is found to be the most important determinant of electricity price, followed by the composition of electricity sales. The chapter

1

also discusses the estimated total elasticities of demand. Estimates obtained by derivation of the reduced-form equation from the structural equations are generally larger in absolute magnitude than those obtained by direct estimation. The estimated total income elasticity of expenditure on electricity is less than unity using either procedure. Estimates of total elasticities of demand obtained using city data are discussed in Appendix 4A.

Chapter 5 discusses the electricity demand models for the commercial and industrial sectors. In both sectors, demand for electricity is specified to be a function of the level of output and of variables affecting the quantity of electricity used per unit of output. Since data are not available on the level of output in the commercial sector, this variable is eliminated by substitution in the demand equation. The empirical results for the commercial sector indicate that the direct long-run elasticity of demand with respect to electricity price is approximately unitary.

The level of output in the industrial sector is measured by value added in manufacturing and the value of mineral production. Value added in manufacturing is treated as an endogenous variable because the level of manufacturing activity in a state will be affected by electricity price. The national own-price elasticity is estimated holding value added in manufacturing constant, and the elasticity for states is estimated allowing value added to vary. The range of estimates for the national elasticity is -1.24 to -1.40, and the range for the state elasticity is -1.53 to -1.75.

The use of duality theory to examine energy substitution in electric power generation and in manufacturing is discussed in Part II. Derivation of the models is discussed in Chapter 6. A normalized restricted profit function is used to derive the model of interfuel substitution in electric power generation. Coal, oil, and gas are treated as variable inputs; and capital, labor, and vintage of capital are treated as fixed inputs. The model of energy substitution in manufacturing is derived using a unit cost function for energy.

Both models permit estimation of all own- and cross-price elasticities of demand for energy inputs subject only to those restrictions implied by economic theory. The models also provide statistical tests of hypotheses concerning other characteristics of the technologies.

The model of interfuel substitution in electric power generation is estimated with cross-section data for individual plants. The empirical results are reported in Chapter 7. The results indicate that electric power generation is characterized by substantial ex post interfuel substitution, homogeneity, absence of strong scale economies, and little embodied technical change. However, weaknesses in the performance of the model indicate the need for caution in interpreting the results.

The model of energy substitution in manufacturing is estimated with *Census of Manufactures* data for two-digit industries for the years 1958, 1962, and 1971. As discussed in Chapter 8, the model performs well for industries accounting for most of the total consumption of energy in manufacturing in each year. The estimated elasticities indicate considerable variation in energy substitution both across industries and across types of energy. Elasticities of demand for aggregate manufacturing are computed as weighted averages of the two-digit industry results. Estimated aggregate own-price elasticities in 1971 are −0.92 for electricity, −2.82 for oil, −1.47 for natural gas, and −1.52 for coal.

Technological change in energy use in manufacturing is tested by pooling data for 1962 and 1971 and performing tests for constancy over time of the parameters of the unit cost function. The null hypothesis of no change in the estimated parameters is rejected for 8 of the 13 industries for which the test can be performed. The hypothesis that the energy-input function is Cobb-Douglas is also tested, and is rejected in 21 of 31 cases.

Time-series data are used to estimate dynamic energy models in Part III. Dynamic models of residential demand for electricity are discussed in Chapter 9. A reduced-form equation for quantity purchased is estimated with typical electric bill data for two alternative dynamic specifications of the demand equation. The results include estimates of short-run total elasticities of demand with respect to electricity price and income for each state.

The estimated income elasticities are surprising in that they are negative for a substantial number of states for both models. Estimates of national short-run elasticities are computed as weighted averages of the results for individual states. For the model that performed best, the estimated national short-run price and income elasticities are −0.58 and −0.18 respectively.

A dynamic model of aggregate energy demand in manufacturing is discussed in Chapter 10. The model provides estimates of the complete time path of the response of energy demand to changes in its own price and in the prices of other inputs. The results also include estimates of the response of demand for each input to temporary excess demands for other inputs.

All estimated short-run price elasticities of demand for energy are statistically significant. The responses to price changes are found to be quite rapid, with the full long-run responses being approximately realized within three years. The estimated long-run own-price elasticity of demand for energy is −0.42. The estimated long-run elasticities of demand for energy with respect to the prices of capital and labor are −0.15 and 0.57 respectively.

**Part I
Long-Run Demand for Electricity**

2

Structure of the Electricity Demand Models

Introduction

The pricing of electricity is different from the pricing of most goods in that the consumer of electricity faces a price schedule rather than a single price. The resulting dependence of price on quantity purchased complicates the estimation and interpretation of elasticities of demand for electricity. The issues raised include the appropriate electricity price data to use in estimating elasticities of demand, the identification of the demand equation, and the distinction between direct and total elasticities of demand.

The issues raised by the dependence of price on quantity purchased are relevant to the design of demand models for all classes of customers. For concreteness, the general structure of the demand models is discussed in the context of residential demand for electricity. The full specification of the residential demand model is discussed in Chapters 3 and 4, and the specifications of the commercial and industrial models are discussed in Chapter 5.

The Dependence of Price on Quantity

The price schedule generally used for electricity is one of declining block rates. The price of the marginal unit purchased is constant within each block of consumption but decreases between blocks. The average price paid for all units is constant and equal to the marginal price only in the first block. After the first block, average price decreases continuously with quantity purchased.[1]

Aggregation of the price schedules of a number of utilities will in general result in a marginal price schedule with more blocks than the schedule for any one utility. Therefore, the price schedule can be more closely approximated by a smooth curve as the level of aggregation increases. In this study, both marginal and average price are treated as smoothly continuous functions of quantity purchased. Since aggregate-state data are used in estimating the price schedules, this approximation should be sufficiently accurate.

A necessary condition for utility maximization is that the consumer equate marginal rates of substitution to ratios of marginal prices. Therefore, marginal rather than average electricity price is the appropriate variable to include in the demand equation to measure the price elasticity of demand. However, marginal price does not incorporate all the relevant information about the price schedule

7

because it does not reflect the amount paid for intramarginal units of consumption, which will have an income effect on the quantity of electricity purchased. Inclusion of a price variable reflecting the cost of intramarginal units in addition to a marginal price variable therefore appears to be desirable.[2]

Practical difficulties are encountered in implementing this "two-price" proposal because the price variables are likely to be highly correlated. One result is that generally only one of the price variables is statistically significant.[3] The multicollinearity introduced by including a second price variable can also be expected to decrease the precision with which the coefficients of other variables are estimated. Therefore, a second price variable is not included in the demand equations estimated here.

In addition to requiring that a choice be made with respect to the price variable, or variables, to be included in the demand equation, the dependence of price on quantity purchased creates a serious identification problem. To illustrate the identification problem, it will be assumed for the moment that the price schedule can be represented as

$$P = d + eQ + v \tag{2.1}$$

where P is marginal price, Q is quantity purchased, e is negative, and v is a disturbance term.[4] It will also be assumed for illustrative purposes that electricity consumption is determined solely by the level of income,

$$Q = a + cY + u \tag{2.2}$$

where Y is income, c is positive, and u is a disturbance term.

Suppose the following "demand equation" is estimated from the data:

$$Q = f + gP + hY + w \tag{2.3}$$

This equation is a linear combination of the true demand and price equations. Estimation of it from the data might yield a high R^2 and a significant negative price elasticity, even though, by construction, demand is perfectly inelastic with respect to price.

To obtain identification of the demand equation, it is necessary to include in the model an equation for the price schedule. The price equation included in the model is

$$P = P(Q, X) \tag{2.4}$$

where X is a vector of the exogenous cost variables that determine the location and shape of the price schedule.

The final difficulty arising from the dependence of price on quantity purchased relates to the interpretation of demand elasticities calculated from the structural demand equation. The coefficients of the demand equation reflect the direct influence of the explanatory variables on quantity purchased. Changes in the explanatory variables will also have indirect effects on the quantity purchased because of the dependence of price on quantity. For example, a change in income will increase the quantity of electricity purchased, resulting in movement along the price schedule and a lower value for electricity price. This in turn will lead to an increase in quantity, further decrease in price, etc. The total effect on quantity purchased of a change in income will be equal to the sum of the direct effect and the whole chain of indirect effects.

Measures of the total response of demand to changes in the explanatory variables are obtained by estimating the reduced-form equation for quantity purchased. Elasticities of demand derived from the reduced-form equation will be referred to as *total elasticities*, and elasticities of demand derived from the structural demand equation will be referred to as *direct elasticities*.[5]

Estimation Procedures

A number of functional forms of the demand and price equations were estimated and the results compared on the basis of goodness of fit and plausibility of the results.[6] The functional forms tested included linear, log-linear, hyperbolic, logarithmic, exponential, and inverse-exponential forms. The performance of the log-linear form was superior, and only this form will be discussed here.

The model consists of a structural demand equation,

$$\ln Q = a_0 + a_1 \ln P + \sum_{i=2}^{m} a_i \ln Z_i + u \tag{2.5}$$

and a structural price equation,

$$\ln P = b_0 + b_1 \ln Q + \sum_{j=2}^{n} b_j \ln X_j + v \tag{2.6}$$

where Q is average quantity purchased per customer, P is the marginal price of electricity, the Z_i and X_i are exogenous variables, and u and v are disturbance terms.

The reduced-form equation for quantity purchased is obtained by substituting for P in equation (2.5),

$$\ln Q = \frac{a_0 + a_1 b_0}{1 - a_1 b_1} + \sum_{i=2}^{m} \frac{a_i}{1 - a_1 b_1} \ln Z_i + \sum_{j=2}^{n} \frac{a_1 b_j}{1 - a_1 b_1} \ln X_j$$
$$+ \frac{u + a_1 v}{1 - a_1 b_1} \tag{2.7}$$

The coefficients of the Z_i variables are equal to the total elasticities of demand. If both a_1 and b_1 are negative and their product is less than unity, as is to be expected, the total elasticities will be larger in absolute magnitude than the direct elasticities.[7]

Given adequate data on marginal price, consistent estimates of all direct elasticities could be obtained by estimating the structural equations by two-stage least squares. Consistent, but not unbiased, estimates of the total elasticities of demand could then be obtained by solving the estimated structural equations for the reduced-form equation for quantity purchased.

Unfortunately, adequate data on marginal electricity price do not exist at the state level. However, data on average price, and on the total cost of various levels of use, do exist and can be used to estimate the direct and total elasticities of demand.

The first step in estimating the model using average price data is to determine the functional relationship between average and marginal price. Equations (2.5) and (2.6) are then estimated using an average price variable in place of marginal price, and the relationship between marginal and average price is used to derive the parameters of the equations that incorporate marginal price.

Substituting average for marginal price in equation (2.6) and taking antilogarithms, the estimated price equation is

$$P_a = b_0 Q^{b_1} \prod_{j=2}^{n} X_j^{b_j} v \tag{2.8}$$

where P_a is the average price of electricity. The relationship between average and marginal price can be derived using the definitional equation for a customer's total bill:

$$P_a Q = \int_{q=0}^{q=Q} P_m dq \tag{2.9}$$

where P_m is the marginal price of electricity. Substituting in equation (2.9) for P_a from equation (2.8), differentiating both sides, and solving for P_a yields

$$P_a = P_m/(1 + b_1) \tag{2.10}$$

Substituting average for marginal price in equation (2.5) and taking antilogarithms, the estimated demand equation is

$$Q = a_0 P_a^{a_1} \prod_{i=2}^{m} Z_i^{a_i} u \tag{2.11}$$

Substituting in equation (2.11) for P_a from equation (2.10) yields

$$Q = a_0 \left(\frac{1}{1 + b_1} \right)^{a_1} P_m{}^{a_1} \prod_{i=2}^{m} Z_i{}^{a_i} u \qquad (2.12)$$

Comparison of equations (2.12) and (2.5) shows that only the intercept term is affected by the use of average price data. Therefore, for the log-linear demand and price equations used here, the estimated elasticities obtained with average price data are identical to those which would be obtained with marginal price data.

Estimates of the total elasticities of demand can be obtained by solving the estimated structural equations for the reduced-form equation for quantity purchased. Alternatively, the reduced-form equation, equation (2.7), can be estimated directly. One shortcoming of the latter approach is that serious multi-collinearity problems are likely to arise as a result of the large number of explanatory variables. Also, since no price variable is included in equation (2.7), this procedure will not yield estimates of the total own-price elasticity.

An alternative method of directly estimating the reduced-form equation is to use typical electric bill (TEB) data, which are indices of the total cost of selected levels of consumption (U.S. Federal Power Commission, various). The data provide direct measures of the location and shape of the price schedule and therefore can be used to replace the vector of exogenous cost variables, X, in equation (2.7).

In order to obtain estimates of the total own-price elasticity, it is desirable to combine the TEB data into a single variable. The reduced-form equation to be estimated is then

$$\ln Q = c_0 + c_1 \ln B + \sum_{i=2}^{m} c_i \ln Z_i + w \qquad (2.13)$$

where B is the TEB variable, w is a disturbance term, c_1 is the total own-price elasticity, and the c_i are the total elasticities with respect to the other variables included in the demand equation.

Since the TEB variable can be expected to be independent of the current value of Q, consistent estimates of the total elasticities can be obtained by estimating equation (2.13) by ordinary least squares. However, the validity of the estimated elasticities will depend on the adequacy of the TEB variable as a proxy for the location and shape of the price schedule. One problem that arises is that the TEB data are fixed-weight indices of the rates charged for electricity purchased for different uses, e.g., lighting and water heating. The weights used are based on "typical" patterns of consumption (U.S. Federal Power Commission, undated). Since the actual pattern of consumption will vary across states, the TEB indices may be poor measures of the actual costs of electricity.

A second problem is that differences in the TEB variable may reflect changes in either the shape or location of the price schedule. Therefore, the effects of changes in the cost of intramarginal units will be confounded with changes in the level of marginal price.[8] For these reasons, greater reliance should be placed on estimated total elasticities of demand derived from the estimated structural equations than on those obtained by direct estimation of the reduced-form equation using TEB data.

Long-Run and Short-Run Elasticities

Since the full response of electricity consumption to a change in an explanatory variable will not be experienced instantaneously, long-run and short-run elasticities of demand will not be equal. In principle, estimates of both the long-run and short-run elasticities could be obtained by estimating dynamic versions of the structural and reduced-form equations with time-series data. However, severe difficulties are encountered in using this approach.

One difficulty is that the length of the available time series is relatively short, limiting the number of explanatory variables that can be included in the model. Also, the existence of strong time trends in many of the relevant variables creates serious multicollinearity problems, especially if more than a few variables are included in the equations. Finally, the existence of regulatory lags of arbitrary length in the response of price schedules to changes in their determinants makes it difficult to obtain reliable estimates of the structural price equation.

For these reasons, it is impractical to estimate the full model using time-series data. However, estimates of short-run total elasticities can be obtained by estimating an abbreviated form of the reduced-form equation with time-series data. Chapter 9 discusses the procedures used and the results. The remainder of this chapter discusses the use of cross-section data to estimate the full model.

Cross-section data offer larger sample sizes and greater independent variation in the explanatory variables. Therefore it is feasible to estimate equations containing as many variables as theory indicates should be included. Interpretation of the time dimension of elasticities of demand estimated with cross-section data depends on the nature of cross-sectional differences in the variables.

If cross-sectional differences in the variables have persisted for many periods, different observational units will either all be in equilibrium or tend to be at the same point of disequilibrium. In this case, elasticities of demand estimated with cross-section data can be interpreted as long-run elasticities. During the 1960s, cross-sectional differences had existed for some time because the variables were largely either constant over time or changing exponentially. By restricting the sample to this period, cross-section analysis can be used to obtain estimates of the long-run elasticities.

The data used are for the 48 contiguous states for the years 1961 through 1969. The cross-section data for individual years are pooled so that the total number of observations in 432. The additional degrees of freedom provided by pooling the data increase the efficiency of the parameter estimates compared to estimates obtained with data for individual years.[9] However, pooling is appropriate only if the parameters of the individual cross-section regressions do not vary over time.

The hypothesis that the parameters are constant over time is tested using an analysis of covariance (Kuh 1963, pp. 118–136). The test statistic is computed as

$$F = \frac{(SSR_p - \sum\limits_{t=1}^{T} SSR_t)/k(T - 1)}{\sum\limits_{t=1}^{T} SSR_t/(n - kT)}$$

where SSR_p = sum of squared residuals from the pooled regression

   SSR_t = sum of squared residuals from the cross-section regression for year t

   T = total number of years

   k = number of parameters estimated

   n = total number of observations

The test statistic is distributed as F with $(kT - k, n - kT)$ degrees of freedom. If the test statistic is not significant, the null hypothesis that the parameters are constant over time need not be rejected.[10] If it is significant, further analyses of covariance can be performed to determine whether the slopes are constant over time and, if they are, to determine whether the intercepts are constant over time.

Dynamic Cross-Section Models

The availability of a rectangular block of data makes it possible to check the assumption that estimates obtained with the static cross-section model can be interpreted as long-run elasticities. The procedure used is to estimate a number of dynamic cross-section models and compare the results for robustness of the estimated long-run elasticities for different dynamic assumptions.[11]

The dynamic models are more expensive in terms of data because they involve lagged values of the explanatory variables in addition to, or in place of, the current values. Therefore, the number of individual cross-sections, or the number of degrees of freedom for a pooled regression, available from the same rectangular block of data is less for dynamic than for static models. In order to compare the results for a number of different dynamic formulations, including ones involving long lags in response, the dynamic models are estimated for only the most recent cross-section.

The specification of the lag structures of dynamic models can be based on theoretical considerations or on ad hoc data fitting. In Chapter 9 the dynamic models implied by a variety of behavioral assumptions are considered. For the present purpose of testing the sensitivity of the estimated long-run elasticities to the dynamic formulation of the model, it is sufficient to consider a number of lag structures that have been widely applied in empirical research.

The simplest type of lag structure is one in which the dependent variable is assumed to respond to a change in an explanatory variable fully in a single period, but only after a delay of one or more periods. Given this assumption, the current values of the explanatory variables should be replaced by their value a period or more earlier. To test the effect of this type of lag structure on the estimated coefficients, separate equations are estimated for the current value of the dependent variable regressed on the values of the explanatory variables lagged one year and lagged two years. In addition, the current value of the dependent variable is correlated with all available past values of the explanatory variables, and a regression is performed in which the lagged value used for each variable is the one having the highest correlation with the dependent variable.

More realistic lag structures allow the response of the dependent variable to be spread over a number of periods. Since the explanatory variables are serially correlated, only a very few lagged values of a given variable can be included in the same equation. However, construction of weighted averages of the current and lagged values allows the testing of the effect of a number of more complex lag structures.[12]

The simplest weighted average is one constructed with equal weights. The weights are given by the formulas

$$W_i = 1/N \quad \text{for } 0 \leqslant i < N$$

$$W_i = 0 \quad \text{for } i \geqslant N$$

where N is the number of values of the variable to be included. Equations in which the current values of all explanatory variables are replaced by simple averages are estimated below for both $N = 5$ and $N = 9$.

If the pattern of response is assumed to have the shape of an inverted V, the appropriate weights are

$$W_i = \frac{a_i}{\sum\limits_{i=0}^{N-1} a_i}$$

where $\quad a_i = 1 + i \quad$ for $0 \leqslant i < (N/2)$

$\qquad a_i = N - i \quad$ for $(N/2) \leqslant i < N$

$\qquad a_i = 0 \qquad$ for $i \geqslant N$

Equations are estimated for $N = 5$ and $N = 9$.

A less restrictive assumption is that the weights follow the Pascal distribution. The general formula for such weights is

$$W_i = \frac{a_i}{\displaystyle\sum_{i=0}^{N-1} a_i} \tag{2.14}$$

where $\quad a_i = \dbinom{r + i - 1}{i} (1 - \lambda)^r \lambda^i \qquad 0 \leqslant i < N$

$\qquad a_i = 0 \qquad\qquad\qquad\qquad\quad i \geqslant N$

For the case in which $r = 1$, the weights decline geometrically:

$$W_i = \frac{(1 - \lambda)}{1 - \lambda^N} \lambda^i \qquad 0 \leqslant i < N$$

$$W_i = 0 \qquad\qquad i \geqslant N$$

Two parameters are now involved in the construction of the weights, N and λ. Equations are estimated for $N = 9$ with $\lambda = 0.4$ and $\lambda = 0.8$.

When $r = 2$, the Pascal distribution weights are given by equation (2.14), with

$$a_i = \frac{r + i - 1}{i} (1 - \lambda)^r \lambda^i \qquad 0 \leqslant i < N$$

$$a_i = 0 \qquad\qquad\qquad\qquad i \geqslant N$$

Again, equations are estimated for $N = 9$ with $\lambda = 0.4$ and $\lambda = 0.8$.

Summary

The structure of the electricity demand models makes it possible to obtain consistent estimates of the elasticities of demand using the available data. The structural demand equation expresses average consumption per customer as a function of marginal price and a number of exogenous variables. The structural price equation expresses marginal price as a function of average consumption and exogenous cost variables. The structural equations are estimated with average price data. For the log-linear demand and price equations used here, the coefficients of all variables in the demand equation are equal for equations estimated with either marginal price or average price.

The estimated coefficients of the structural demand equation are equal to the estimated direct elasticities of demand. The direct elasticities do not measure the total response of consumption to changes in the variables because they do not include the indirect effects arising from the dependence of price on quantity purchased. Estimates of the total elasticities of demand are equal to the estimated coefficients of the reduced-form equation for quantity purchased. The estimated reduced-form equation can be obtained by solution of the estimated structural equations or by direct estimation using typical electric bill (TEB) data. Results obtained using the former approach are considered to be more reliable.

The residential model is estimated with pooled cross-section state data for the years 1961 through 1969. The estimated elasticities are interpreted as long-run elasticities. The validity of this interpretation is checked by estimating a number of dynamic cross-section models.

Notes

1. For utilities that impose a fixed customer charge, average price will differ from marginal price, and will decrease with quantity purchased, in the first block as well as in later blocks.

2. See Taylor (1975), and Acton, Mitchell, and Mowill (1976). These studies also point out that the use of declining block rates results in a demand correspondence rather than a demand function. However, this is not likely to cause practical difficulties when aggregate data are used.

3. See Acton, Mitchell, and Mowill (1976), and Meyer (1976).

4. The price schedule for a single utility is nonstochastic. However, when state data are used, it is useful to treat the aggregate price schedule as a stochastic equation whose parameters are to be estimated.

5. The total elasticity of demand with respect to electricity price measures the effect on demand of a parallel shift in the rate schedule. A change in the slope of the rate schedule would affect the total elasticities of demand for all variables.

6. See Halvorsen (1972) for discussion of the procedures used.

7. The use of inverted rate schedules, in which price is an increasing function of quantity purchased, has sometimes been suggested as a means of reducing the demand for electricity. The use of inverted rate schedules would result in the total elasticities of demand being smaller in absolute magnitude than the direct elasticities. The net result on the rate of growth of electricity demand cannot be determined a priori.

8. As discussed in Chapter 9, the problems involved in the use of a TEB variable should be less serious for time-series data.

9. However, to the extent that the variables are constant, or changing exponentially, over time, the effective increase in the number of degrees of freedom is overstated by the increase in the number of observations.

10. Since the desired result is that the null hypothesis not be rejected, the required significance level for F should not be set too high.

11. Unlike the dynamic time-series models used in Chapter 9, the dynamic cross-section models do not yield estimates of short-run elasticities.

12. The estimation of various dynamic formulations using weighted averages is discussed in Griliches (1967), pp. 25–26.

3

Residential Electricity Demand Equation

Introduction

The residential demand equation is estimated with a rectangular block of data for the 48 contiguous states for the years 1961 through 1969. A static formulation of the demand equation is estimated with cross-section data for each year, as well as with a pooled sample of data for all years. An analysis of covariance indicates that the parameters are constant over time and, therefore, that pooling of the data for all years is appropriate.

The estimate of the own-price elasticity of demand obtained with the pooled sample is −1.15. The estimated income elasticity is 0.51, and the estimated elasticity of demand with respect to gas price is 0.04. The estimated elasticities are interpreted as measures of the long-run responses of electricity demand to changes in the explanatory variables. To test the robustness of the estimated long-run elasticities, a number of dynamic formulations of the demand equation are also estimated. The range of estimated elasticities is −1.00 to −1.21 for electricity price, 0.48 to 0.54 for income, and 0.05 to 0.08 for gas price.

The large number of observations available for the pooled sample permits estimation of separate demand equations for four geographic areas. The results indicate significant differences in the characteristics of demand across regions. The sample is also disaggregated on the basis of the level of electricity price. The results provide little support for the hypothesis that the own-price elasticity of demand is an increasing function of the level of electricity price.

Specification of the Demand Function

Residential electricity demand can be expected to be a function of both economic and noneconomic variables. Relevant economic variables include the price of electricity, the prices of substitutes and complements, and the level of income. Noneconomic determinants of electricity demand include climate, demographic variables, and the characteristics of the housing stock.

The specification of the residential demand equation is summarized in Table 3-1. The dependent variable is average annual sales per customer. The electricity price variable included in the equation is the average price per kilowatt-hour. The most important substitute for electricity in the residential sector is gas.

19

Table 3-1
Specification of the Residential Demand Equation

$$\ln Q_R = \alpha_Q + \alpha_E \ln P_R + \alpha_Y \ln Y + \alpha_G \ln G_R + \alpha_A \ln A + \alpha_D \ln D + \alpha_J \ln J$$
$$+ \alpha_U \ln U + \alpha_M \ln M + \alpha_H \ln H + \alpha_T T + u_R$$

where Q_R = average annual residential electricity sales per customer, in thousands of kWh

P_R = average real price of residential electricity, in cents per kWh

Y = average real income per capita, in thousands of dollars

G_R = average real gas price for all types of gas, in cents per therm

A = index of real wholesale prices of selected electric appliances

D = heating degree days

J = average July temperature, in degrees Fahrenheit

U = percentage of population living in rural areas

M = percentage of housing units in multiunit structures

H = average size of households

T = time

u = a disturbance term

Since both utility and nonutility gas compete with electricity, the gas price variable included in the equation is the average price of all types of residential gas.

Fuel oil also competes with electricity in the home heating market, but the price of fuel oil cannot be included in the equation because adequate data are not available for it. The percent of housing units with oil heat was experimented with as a proxy variable for the price of fuel oil, but the results did not justify including this variable in the equation.

The most important complements of electricity are electric appliances. Cross-section data on appliance prices are not available. However, cross-sectional variation in appliances prices is probably not very great, nor highly correlated with the included variables. Therefore, the inability to include a variable for cross-sectional differences in appliance prices should not result in serious biases in the estimated coefficients.

Changes in electric appliance prices over time will be more important than cross-sectional differences. The most appropriate appliance price variable would be a weighted average index of the retail prices of all electric appliances, the weights being based on the electricity requirements of each appliance under normal use. Unfortunately, the only data available are wholesale price indices for a limited number of appliances, with the weights used being based on the value of sales rather than on electricity requirements. A variable for electric appliance prices is constructed from the available data but is expected to contain large measurement errors.

The prices of gas appliances should also affect electricity demand but could not be included in the equation because of a lack of data. Cross-sectional variation in the prices of gas appliances should not be very great. Changes in gas appliance prices over time are probably more important. To the extent that changes over time are trend-like, they will be reflected by the included trend variable.

The income variable included in the demand equation is average per capita income. Data on median family income are also available, but only for census years. Average per capita income is a better index of the standard of living in each state than median family income because it is not affected by average family size.

The economic variables included in the demand equation are deflated by the national consumer price index. The data are not deflated for cross-sectional differences in the general price level. The effects of not adjusting for cross-sectional differences in the price level can be analyzed using Theil's formula for specification error (Theil 1957).

The expected value of the estimate of the coefficient of variable i in an equation that omits one or more relevant variables is

$$E(b_i) = B_i + \sum_{j=1}^{n} a_{ij}B_j \tag{3.1}$$

where $E(b_i)$ = the expected value of the estimate of the coefficient of variable i obtained from the misspecified model

B_i = the coefficient of variable i in a correctly specified model

a_{ij} = the expected value of the coefficient of variable i in an auxilliary regression of excluded variable j on the included variables

B_j = the coefficient of excluded variable j in a correctly specified model

The true demand equation is assumed to be

$$\ln Q = a + c_1(\ln P - \ln X) + c_2(\ln Y - \ln X) + c_3(\ln G - \ln X) + u \tag{3.2}$$

where P = nominal electricity price

Y = nominal income

G = nominal gas price

X = an index of cross-sectional differences in the general price level

The inclusion of noneconomic variables would not affect the analysis, since they would not involve X.

Instead of equation (3.2), an equation incorporating the undeflated values of the variables is estimated. This is equivalent to the specification error of omitting variable X, which has the coefficient $-(c_1 + c_2 + c_3)$. From equation (3.1), the expected value of the coefficients estimated for the misspecified equation is

$$E(b_i) = B_i - a_{ix}(c_1 + c_2 + c_3)$$

where a_{ix} is the coefficient of variable i in the auxilliary regression of X on the included variables. The coefficients a_{ix} can be expected to be positive for electricity price, gas price, and income because the nominal value of all three will tend to be higher in areas for which the general price level is higher. The sign of the specification bias for these variables will therefore depend on the sign of $-(c_1 + c_2 + c_3)$.

The electricity price coefficient, c_1, should be negative, and the other coefficients positive. Therefore, the expected value of the specification bias, s, will be,

$$E(s) > 0 \quad \text{if } |c_1| > |c_2 + c_3|$$
$$E(s) = 0 \quad \text{if } |c_1| = |c_2 + c_3|$$
$$E(s) < 0 \quad \text{if } |c_1| < |c_2 + c_3|$$

The regression results discussed below indicate that c_1 is larger in absolute value than the sum of c_2 and c_3, so the expected specification bias will be positive. The use of cross-section data that are not deflated for differences in the general price level should result in the estimated coefficient of electricity price being biased toward zero and the estimated coefficients of income and gas price being biased away from zero. In order to reduce the magnitude of the biases, data for Hawaii and Alaska are excluded from the sample to reduce the cross-sectional variation in price levels.

Variables for July temperature and heating degree days are included among the noneconomic variables in the demand equation as measures of home cooling and heating requirements respectively. Electricity is the dominant energy source for home cooling. Since the demand for home cooling will be positively related to summer temperature, the coefficient of the July temperature variable in the estimated demand equation should be positive.

The relationship between electricity demand and home heating requirements is less clear. Both gas and fuel oil are potential substitutes for electricity in home heating. Electric home heating is characterized by lower capital costs and higher operating costs than its competitors. As total heating requirements increase, operating costs become more important, and therefore the total cost of electric home heating becomes less competitive. As a result, the coefficient of the heating degree days variable may have either a positive or a negative sign in the estimated demand equation.

Residential electricity demand can be expected to differ for rural and urban customers because of differences in the availability of substitutes for domestic energy use, as well as differences in the availability of alternative energy sources. Therefore, a variable for the percent of population living in rural areas is included in the demand equation and is expected to have a positive coefficient.

Customers who live in apartments are likely to consume less electricity than those who live in single-family structures. The smaller size of apartments both reduces the need for electricity for some purposes and restricts the customer's ability to acquire large electric appliances. A variable for the percent of housing units in multiunit structures is included in the demand equation to measure the effect of apartment living on residential demand. The apartment variable should have a negative coefficient, but the full effect of differences in the type of housing will be obscured because some apartment dwellers are served under commercial rates.

Household size, measured by the number of people per household, may also affect electricity demand. Large families will tend to own more appliances and to use them more intensively. The net effect on electricity demand is not clear, because more intensive utilization raises the relative cost of electric appliances. Large families may own more appliances in total but fewer electric appliances.

Several time-related variables cannot be included explicitly in the demand equation. These include the prices of gas appliances, the invention and diffusion of new types of electric appliances, changes in the efficiency with which existing types of electric appliances use energy, and changes in attitudes toward energy conservation. A time-trend term is included in the equation to serve as a proxy for omitted time-related variables.

Edison Electric Institute (various) data are used to calculate average annual electricity sales per customer and the average price of electricity. Income per capita data are from U.S. Department of Commerce (various). The average price of gas data are calculated from American Gas Association (various).

U.S. Bureau of Labor Statistics (various) data are used in constructing an index of the wholesale prices of electric appliances. The household appliance index provided by the Bureau of Labor Statistics includes all types of ranges and ovens, including nonelectric ones. Therefore, the index for ranges and ovens is subtracted from the household appliances index, and the index for electric ranges is added back in. The modified household appliances index is then averaged with the index for televisions, radios, and phonographs. In all calculations the indices are weighted by value-of-sale weights provided in U.S. Bureau of Labor Statistics (various).

The percentage of population living in rural areas is calculated from data in U.S. Bureau of the Census (various). The data are for 1960 and 1970 only. Data are obtained for the intermediate years by linear interpolation. Similarly, data on the percentage of housing units in multiunit structures are interpolated from data appearing in U.S. Bureau of the Census (1960, 1970). The change in both variables over the 10 years is not great, so the use of linear interpolation should not cause significant errors.

Average size of household is calculated as population divided by the number of households. Data on population and number of households are from U.S. Bureau of the Census (various). Data on number of households are not available for 1961-1964 nor for 1969. Therefore, linear interpolation is used to obtain these data.

Data on heating degree days and average July temperatures, both 30-year averages for 1931-1960, are reported for a large number of cities in U.S. Bureau of the Census (1962). To obtain data for states, a weighted average of the data for the three largest cities for which data are available is calculated, using city populations as the weights. The climate variables are assumed to be constant over the period studied. This would be incorrect for national data because of population movements between areas with different climates, but this effect should not be serious for intrastate averages.

The structural demand equation is estimated by two-stage least squares. In the first stage the endogenous price variable is regressed on all the exogenous variables in the model. The exogenous variables appearing in the price equation are shown in Table 4-1. Briefly, they are wage costs, fuel costs, ratio of industrial to residential sales, type of ownership, percent rural population, time, and the consumer price index.

The use of average data for states may result in heteroscedasticity of the disturbance term. A procedure commonly used to correct heteroscedasticity resulting from the use of averaged data is to weight all observations by the number of customers in each state. Weighted and unweighted regressions are compared using the tests proposed by Goldfeld and Quandt (1965). The tests indicate that the unweighted regressions perform best, and only those results are reported here.

Empirical Results: Static Model

As discussed in Chapter 2, a number of functional forms of the static demand equation were estimated and compared on the bases of goodness of fit and plausibility of the results. The performance of the log-linear form was superior, and only these results are reported here.[1]

The estimates of the parameters obtained with the pooled cross-section sample are shown in Table 3-2. The coefficients of electricity price, electric appliance price, and percent of housing units in multiunit structures have the expected negative signs. The signs of the coefficients of income, gas price, July temperature, and percent rural population are positive as expected. The signs of the effects of heating degree days, household size, and time are not clear a priori. The estimated coefficients of these variables are all negative.

Since the demand equation is log-linear, the estimated coefficients are equal to the estimated direct elasticities of demand, which indicate the direct response of electricity demand to changes in the explanatory variables. They do not indicate the total response because they do not include the indirect effects on demand that result from the dependence of price on quantity purchased. Estimates of the total elasticities of demand are discussed in Chapter 4.

The estimated direct own-price elasticity is −1.14 and is both highly significant and significantly greater than one in absolute magnitude. The estimated direct income elasticity of 0.52 is highly significant and significantly less than one.[2] The estimated cross-elasticity of demand with respect to gas price is significant but surprisingly small at 0.05.[3]

The estimated coefficients of the variables for both electric appliance price and percent of housing units in multiunit structures have the expected negative

Table 3-2
Estimates of Parameters of the Residential Demand Equation: Pooled Sample[a]

Parameter	Estimate	Standard Error	Significance Level[b]
α_Q	−0.514	0.600	.392
α_E	−1.138	0.036	.0001
α_Y	0.520	0.063	.0001
α_G	0.047	0.018	.008
α_A	−0.347	0.644	.589
α_D	−0.022	0.019	.238
α_J	0.522	0.118	.0001
α_U	0.205	0.026	.0001
α_M	−0.020	0.029	.501
α_H	−0.238	0.122	.052
α_T	−0.021	0.022	.328
R^2 = 0.917			

[a]The number of observations is 432.
[b]Significance level for a two-tailed test based on the normal distribution. A significance level of .0001 indicates that the estimated parameter is significant at this level or above.

signs but are insignificant. The insignificance of these variables is due in part to measurement problems. The electric appliance price variable does not include all major appliances, refers to wholesale rather than retail prices, and is weighted by value of sales rather than electricity usage. The housing variable is an adequate measure of the importance of apartments in the housing market, but the phenomena it is intended to reflect are obscured by the omission from residential sales figures of some sales to apartment buildings.

The estimated demand equation with the appliance price and housing structure variables omitted is

$$\ln Q_R = -0.594 - 1.148 \ln P_R + 0.513 \ln Y + 0.040 \ln G_R$$
$$\quad\quad (0.585) \quad (0.034) \quad\quad\quad (0.063) \quad\quad\quad (0.015)$$

$$- 0.024 \ln D + 0.539 \ln J + 0.214 \ln U - 0.241 \ln H$$
$$(0.018) \quad\quad\quad (0.117) \quad\quad\quad (0.020) \quad\quad\quad (0.123)$$

$$- 0.111\, T \quad R^2 = 0.915 \quad (3.3)$$
$$(0.003)$$

where the figures in parentheses are estimated standard errors. The estimated parameters are very similar to those in Table 3-2. The principal difference is that the coefficient of time, a_T, becomes smaller in absolute magnitude but highly significant.[4] The value of a_T is equal to the estimated exponential rate of growth in demand resulting from variables not included explicitly in the demand equation. The estimated growth rate is −1 percent per year.

Since the appliance price and housing structure variables are not significant, and their omission has negligible effects on most of the remaining estimated parameters, they are omitted from further demand equations estimated in this chapter. The coefficient of heating degree days is also not significant in the log-linear demand equation. However, it is significant in some of the other functional forms estimated, and the omission of this variable has substantial effects on the estimates of some of the remaining parameters. Therefore the heating degree days variable is retained in the demand equation.

The estimated elasticities of demand indicate the responsiveness of electricity demand to each of the explanatory variables but do not indicate how important each variable is in terms of its contribution to the variation across observations in the amount of electricity consumed. A variable with a high elasticity but a low variance might contribute only slightly to differences in electricity consumption between observations. One measure of the importance of an explanatory variable is the beta coefficient, which indicates the effect on demand of a typical change in the variable. The formula for the beta coefficient (Goldberger 1964, pp. 197-198) is

$$B_j = b_j \frac{S_j}{S_Q}$$

where B_j = the beta coefficient for variable j

        b_j = the estimated coefficient of variable j

        S_j = the standard deviation of variable j

        S_Q = the standard deviation of the dependent variable

The beta coefficients for equation (3.3) are shown in Table 3–3.

Electricity price is clearly the most important determinant of differences in electricity demand in the sample. The beta coefficient for electricity price is almost three times as large as that for income, which is the second most important variable. Although the elasticity of demand with respect to July temperature is as large as the income elasticity of demand, the beta coefficient for July temperature is much lower because the standard deviation of this variable is small.

The preceding results are for the pooled sample. Pooling of cross-section data for more than one year is permissible only if the parameters are constant over time. As discussed in Chapter 2, constancy of the parameters can be tested by estimating equations for each cross-section and performing an analysis of covariance.

The analysis of covariance is performed for the demand equation with the housing and appliance price variables omitted. The estimated parameters for each year are shown in Table 3–4. Casual inspection of the results indicates that the parameters have changed over time. The estimated coefficient of electricity price fluctuates somewhat from year to year, but there appears to be an upward trend in its absolute value over time. Similarly, it appears that the gas price and

Table 3–3
Beta Coefficients for the Residential Demand Equation

Variable	Beta Coefficient
P_R	0.959
Y	0.316
G_R	0.048
D	0.037
J	0.107
U	0.289
H	0.040
T	0.085

Table 3–4
Estimates of Parameters of the Residential Demand Equation: Individual Cross-Sections[a]

Year				Parameter					
	α_Q	α_E	α_Y	α_G	α_D	α_J	α_U	α_H	R^2
1961	0.222	−1.138	0.514	0.043	0.004	0.213	0.245	−0.080	0.879
1962	0.395	−1.058	0.740	0.022	−0.074	0.186	0.324	0.046	0.905
1963	0.103	−1.085	0.638	0.029	−0.049	0.312	0.284	−0.152	0.885
1964	−0.149	−1.145	0.445	0.027	−0.010	0.462	0.217	−0.389	0.876
1965	−0.045	−1.120	0.541	0.033	−0.038	0.435	0.227	−0.332	0.887
1966	−1.090	−1.183	0.490	0.053	−0.022	0.675	0.177	−0.281	0.872
1967	−1.067	−1.159	0.448	0.065	−0.013	0.690	0.167	−0.392	0.875
1968	−2.373	−1.218	0.437	0.065	−0.001	0.960	0.157	−0.301	0.884
1969	−2.463	−1.246	0.485	0.054	−0.017	1.001	0.179	−0.338	0.891

[a]The number of observations for each cross-section is 48.

July temperature coefficients have increased over time and the estimated coefficients of the income and rural population variables have decreased. The apparent decrease in the intercept term is a reflection of time-related variables that are not included explicitly in the equation but that are represented by the time-trend term in the pooled regression.

Despite these apparent changes, the hypothesis that the parameters are constant over time is not rejected statistically. The value of the test statistic is 0.27, whereas the critical value at the 10 percent level is 1.24. Therefore, pooling of the data for different years is appropriate.

Empirical Results: Dynamic Models

Elasticities of demand calculated from the static model can be interpreted as long-run elasticities if there are no lags in the response of the dependent variable or if current differences in the explanatory variables across states also represent long-run differences. It would not be realistic to assume that there are no lags in the response of electricity consumption to changes in the explanatory variables, since the response may involve the acquisition of major appliances. However, during the sample period, current differences in the explanatory variables probably did reflect long-run differences quite accurately.

To check the assumption that the coefficients of the static model do reflect long-run relationships, the demand equation is estimated for a variety of dynamic models. If the estimated coefficients do not differ significantly in the static and dynamic models, the elasticities of demand calculated from the static model can be considered to be robust measures of the long-run response of consumption to the explanatory variables.

The dynamic formulations include both simple lags and distributed lags. For the latter, weighted averages over time are constructed using equal weights, inverted-V distributions, and first- and second-order Pascal distributions. The calculation of the weighted averages is discussed in Chapter 2. The dynamic demand equations are estimated for the 1969 cross-section.

The estimation results for the simple lag formulations of the demand equation are shown in Table 3-5 together with the static 1969 cross-section regression (the case of zero lags). Table 3-6 shows the regression results for the distributed lag models.

All dynamic estimates of the own-price elasticity lie within the range -1.00 to -1.21. As shown in equation (3.3), the corresponding estimate obtained for the static model using the pooled sample is -1.15. The range of dynamic income elasticities is 0.48 to 0.54, compared to an estimate of 0.51 for the static model. The range for the estimated cross-elasticities with respect to gas price of 0.05 to 0.08 is somewhat higher than the estimate of 0.04 obtained with the static model, but the differences are small relative to the estimated standard errors.

Table 3-5
Residential Demand Equation with Lagged Explanatory Variables[a]

Periods Lagged[b]	Parameter								
	α_Q	α_E	α_Y	α_G	α_D	α_J	α_U	α_H	R^2
0	-2.463 (1.79)	-1.246[c] (0.122)	0.485[c] (0.206)	0.054 (0.055)	-0.017 (0.060)	1.001[c] (0.357)	0.179[c] (0.069)	-0.338 (0.376)	0.891
1	-2.568 (1.82)	-1.165[c] (0.120)	0.491[c] (0.199)	0.071 (0.053)	-0.032 (0.058)	1.061[c] (0.365)	0.182[c] (0.070)	-0.378 (0.362)	0.889
2	-2.206 (1.59)	-1.101[c] (0.089)	0.501[c] (0.183)	0.080[c] (0.045)	-0.055 (0.050)	1.027[c] (0.316)	0.201[c] (0.062)	-0.431 (0.327)	0.910
Mixed	-2.220 (1.70)	-1.170[c] (0.101)	0.478[c] (0.191)	0.048 (0.049)	-0.032 (0.054)	0.958[c] (0.341)	0.185[c] (0.065)	-0.308 (0.350)	0.897

[a]Figures in parentheses are estimated standard errors.
[b]All explanatory variables are lagged the same number of periods except in the mixed equation, in which Y and H are lagged one period, G is lagged two periods, and all other variables are not lagged.
[c]Significant at the .05 level.

Table 3-6
Residential Demand Equation with Distributed Lags[a]

Equation[b]	Parameter								R^2
	α_Q	α_E	α_Y	α_G	α_D	α_J	α_U	α_H	
1st Order Pascal, λ = 0.8	-1.745 (1.59)	-1.079[c] (0.094)	0.536[c] (0.186)	0.068 (0.052)	-0.074 (0.052)	0.909[c] (0.320)	0.228[c] (0.064)	-0.326 (0.345)	0.909
1st Order Pascal, λ = 0.4	-2.378 (1.74)	-1.197[c] (0.114)	0.499[c] (0.199)	0.061 (0.052)	-0.031 (0.057)	1.005[c] (0.348)	0.187[c] (0.067)	-0.352 (0.365)	0.896
2nd Order Pascal, λ = 0.8	-1.309 (1.54)	-1.003[c] (0.087)	0.533[c] (0.179)	0.074[c] (0.039)	-0.100[c] (0.049)	0.847[c] (0.309)	0.253[c] (0.064)	-0.328 (0.340)	0.913
2nd Order Pascal, λ = 0.4	-1.893 (1.82)	-1.210[c] (0.114)	0.475[c] (0.208)	0.057 (0.053)	-0.013 (0.059)	0.865[c] (0.364)	0.176[c] (0.071)	-0.342 (0.382)	0.885
5-Year Invert. V	-2.045 (1.64)	-1.111[c] (0.098)	0.515[c] (0.187)	0.075 (0.046)	-0.057 (0.053)	0.972[c] (0.327)	0.205[c] (0.064)	-0.369 (0.340)	0.906
9-Year Invert. V	-1.297 (1.54)	-1.005[c] (0.087)	0.534[c] (0.178)	0.076[c] (0.039)	-0.098[c] (0.050)	0.841[c] (0.309)	0.250[c] (0.063)	-0.323 (0.336)	0.913
5-Year Simp. Av.	-1.944 (1.63)	-1.110[c] (0.098)	0.525[c] (0.187)	0.072 (0.046)	-0.060 (0.053)	0.945[c] (0.326)	0.210[c] (0.064)	-0.348 (0.341)	0.906
9-Year Simp. Av.	-1.345 (1.54)	-1.011[c] (0.088)	0.534[c] (0.180)	0.073[c] (0.040)	-0.098[c] (0.050)	0.851[c] (0.310)	0.252[c] (0.064)	-0.326 (0.343)	0.913

[a]Figures in parentheses are estimated standard errors.
[b]The number of observations for each equation is 48.
[c]Significant at the .05 level.

Comparison of the static results with those obtained with alternative dynamic formulations of the demand equation indicates that the static model is appropriate for estimating long-run elasticities for the period covered by the sample. An advantage of using the static model rather than the dynamic models is that it is much less expensive in terms of data. The total available degrees of freedom for the static model is 432, compared to 48 for the dynamic model. The large number of degrees of freedom available for the static model makes it possible to disaggregate the sample in potentially interesting ways, as discussed in the following section.

Empirical Results: Disaggregated Samples

Estimation of a single demand equation for the 48 contiguous states implies that the characteristics of demand are the same in all the states. In order to test for differences in elasticities of demand across geographic areas, separate regressions are performed for four areas. The estimated parameters for each area are shown in Table 3-7. The census regions comprising each area are listed in the table notes.

An analysis of covariance rejects the null hypothesis that all parameters are constant across geographic areas but does not indicate which parameters are responsible for the rejection. As shown in Table 3-7, the estimated own-price elasticities for the East, South, and West are very similar to the national estimate, but the absolute magnitude of the estimate for the North is considerably smaller. All estimates of the own-price elasticity are highly significant. The estimated income elasticities for the East and South are highly significant and similar to the national estimate, but the estimates for the North and West are small and not statistically significant. The estimated elasticities of demand with respect to gas price are considerably larger than the national estimate for the South and West and are small and insignificant for the East and North. The coefficient of the time variable is significant and negative for the East, significant and positive for the North, and insignificant for the South and West.

Disaggregation of the sample can also be used to test whether elasticities of demand are functions of the values of the explanatory variables. Of particular interest is the assertion frequently made in policy discussions that the own-price elasticity of demand is positively related to the level of electricity price. The rationale for this assertion is that at low electricity price levels people do not notice, or do not choose to respond to, changes in price. While the theoretical basis for this assumption is dubious, the assertion has received sufficient attention to warrant empirical testing.

In order to test for a relationship between the own-price elasticity and the level of electricity price, the sample is disaggregated into low-price and high-price subsamples. The disaggregation is based on the average value of electricity price

Table 3-7
Residential Demand Equation: Disaggregation by Geographic Area[a]

Parameter	East[b]	South[c]	North[d]	West[e]
α_Q	−1.926	−2.478	−2.095	−3.534[f]
	(1.92)	(1.90)	(4.52)	(0.378)
α_E	−1.154[f]	−1.054[f]	−0.704[f]	−1.082[f]
	(0.073)	(0.026)	(0.102)	(0.048)
α_Y	0.461[f]	0.517[f]	0.032	0.034
	(0.059)	(0.116)	(0.088)	(0.083)
α_G	−0.004	0.288[f]	−0.012	0.190[f]
	(0.017)	(0.034)	(0.041)	(0.046)
α_D	0.231[f]	−0.010	0.195	0.059[f]
	(0.076)	(0.025)	(0.152)	(0.022)
α_J	0.326	0.828[f]	0.311	1.318[f]
	(0.308)	(0.408)	(0.745)	(0.099)
α_U	0.120[f]	0.308[f]	0.284[f]	0.148[f]
	(0.020)	(0.066)	(0.039)	(0.027)
α_H	0.150	−0.175	0.058	−0.946[f]
	(0.238)	(0.169)	(0.244)	(0.186)
α_T	−0.012[f]	0.008	0.021[f]	(0.0003)
	(0.004)	(0.005)	(0.006)	(0.003)
R^2	0.966	0.984	0.975	0.990
Number of Observations	126	108	63	99

[a]Figures in parentheses are estimated standard errors.
[b]New England, Middle Atlantic, and East North Central regions.
[c]South Atlantic and East South Central regions.
[d]West North Central region.
[e]Mountain and Pacific regions
[f]Significant at the .05 level.

during the period for each state, so the same states appear in a given subsample in each year.

The estimated parameters for the low-price and high-price subsamples are shown in Table 3-8. An analysis of covariance rejects the null hypothesis that all parameters are equal in the two samples. However, the difference in the estimated own-price elasticities is not large. The estimated elasticity is −1.22 for the low-price sample and −1.36 for the high-price sample. Differences in the estimated elasticities of demand with respect to income, heating degree days, July temperature, and percent rural population are larger both in absolute terms and relative to their estimated standard errors.

Since it is implausible that the nonprice elasticities depend on the level of electricity price, the differences in the results for the two samples presumably

Table 3-8
Residential Demand Equation: Disaggregation by Value of Electricity Price

Parameter	Low-Price Sample		High-Price Sample	
	Estimate	Standard Error	Estimate	Standard Error
α_Q	−2.083	0.742	−5.492	1.510
α_E	−1.216	0.050	−1.357	0.147
α_Y	0.510	0.122	0.184	0.078
α_G	−0.123	0.035	−0.002	0.016
α_D	−0.016	0.028	0.206	0.043
α_J	0.924	0.164	1.183	0.245
α_U	0.118	0.044	0.129	0.028
α_H	−0.292	0.226	0.570	0.157
α_T	−0.012	0.006	−0.006	0.006
	R^2 = 0.909		R^2 = 0.862	

reflect something other than differences in the price of electricity. One possibility is that differences in the elasticities actually reflect geographic differences, since the level of electricity price tends to vary by region.[5]

While the hypothesis that the own-price elasticity is a function of the level of electricity price receives little empirical support, the opposing hypothesis that all elasticities are constant in the relevant range does receive support. Since the log-linear functional form for the demand equation imposes constancy on the estimated elasticities, its superior performance relative to functional forms that do not do so indicates that the elasticities are in fact constant. Also, acceptance of the null hypothesis that the parameters of the demand equation are constant over time implies that the elasticities are also constant over time, despite changes in the values of the explanatory variables.

Concluding Comments

The estimates of the long-run elasticities of demand for electricity in the residential sector are very robust. Electricity price is a highly significant determinant of electricity consumption, and the own-price elasticity is greater than unity in absolute magnitude. The estimated income elasticity is both highly significant and significantly less than one. The estimated elasticity with respect to the price of gas is significant but surprisingly small.

Estimation of ths structural demand equation yields estimates of the direct elasticities of demand. The direct elasticities do not measure the total response of electricity demand to changes in the explanatory variables because they do not include the indirect effects on demand that result from the dependence of price on quantity purchased. Estimates of the total elasticities of demand are discussed in the next chapter.

Notes

1. Results for other functional forms are discussed in Halvorsen (1972).

2. The estimated direct income elasticity does not indicate the distributional effects of policies affecting electricity price. Distributional effects depend on the total income elasticity of demand and the total income elasticity of expenditure on electricity, which are discussed in Chapter 4.

3. The estimated cross-price elasticity obtained with city data shows somewhat more responsiveness of electricity demand to gas price, see Appendix 4A.

4. The standard error of a_T is reduced because the time and appliance price variables are highly correlated. Omitting time from the equation makes appliance price significant, but with a positive sign, because of the omission of other time-related factors. Therefore, it was decided to omit appliance price and retain time.

5. Of course, it is also possible that the apparent geographical differences in the elasticities are actually due to variation in the values of the variables, but this seems unlikely for the reasons discussed below.

4 Residential Electricity Price and Reduced-Form Equations

Introduction

The dependence of price on quantity purchased requires the use of a simultaneous model incorporating both demand and price equations. The price equation is also of interest for its own sake because it indicates the effect on electricity price of changes in each cost component.

The empirical results indicate that quantity purchased is the most important determinant of electricity price. The composition of electricity sales, measured by the ratio of industrial to residential sales, is next most important. Fuel costs have a surprisingly small effect on electricity price. The parameters of the price equation appear to be constant over time, but to differ across geographic areas.

Elasticities of demand estimated with a structural demand equation measure the direct effects of the explanatory variables on consumption. The total response of consumption to changes in the explanatory variables will include indirect effects arising from the dependence of price on quantity purchased. Estimates of the total elasticities of demand are obtained from the reduced-form equation for quantity purchased. The reduced-form equation can be derived from the estimated structural equations or estimated directly using typical electric bill (TEB) data.[1]

The estimated total elasticities of demand are quite sensitive to the method used to obtain them. The estimates derived from the structural equations are generally larger in absolute magnitude than those obtained by direct estimation of the reduced-form equation. Estimates of total elasticities of demand obtained by estimation of the reduced-form equation with city data are discussed in Appendix 4A.

Specification of the Price Equation

The price paid by a residential electricity customer depends on the location and shape of the price schedule and the quantity of electricity purchased. The location and shape of the price schedule will be determined by the utility's average and marginal costs, which in turn will be determined by the prices of labor, capital, and fuel used in generation, the costs of inputs required for transmission and distribution, and the composition of sales.

The specification of the price equation is summarized in Table 4-1. The dependent variable is the average price of electricity. The quantity of electricity purchased is equal to average annual sales per residential customer. The price of labor is approximated by average hourly earnings in manufacturing.

Because of the capital intensive nature of electricity production and distribution, capital costs are an important determinant of electricity price. Since public-owned utilities have significantly different capital costs than do investor-owned utilities, the price equation includes a variable for the percent of generation produced by public-owned utilities. The coefficient of this variable is expected to be negative, reflecting both the lower cost of capital to public-owned utilities and their lower tax obligations.

The fuel cost variable included in the equation is equal to the average cost of fuel per kilowatt-hour produced from nonhydroelectric sources times the percentage of generation from these sources. Thus, it is equal to the cost of fuel per kilowatt-hour of total generation.

Distribution costs per customer can be expected to be related to population density. The amount of physical capital (e.g., miles of distribution lines) and labor required to service each customer will be less the closer together customers are located. However, the cost of these inputs may be higher in densely settled

Table 4-1
Specification of the Residential Price Equation

$$\ln N_R = \beta_N + \beta_Q \ln Q_R + \beta_W \ln W + \beta_K \ln K + \beta_F \ln F + \beta_U \ln U$$
$$+ \beta_I \ln I + \beta_T T + u$$

$$P_R = N_R / X$$

where N_R = average nominal price of electricity, in cents per kWh

Q_R = average annual residential electricity sales per customer, in thousands of kWh

L = average hourly earnings in manufacturing, in cents

K = percentage of generation produced by public-owned utilities

F = cost of fuel per kWh of generation, in hundredths of a cent

U = percentage of population living in rural areas

I = ratio of total industrial sales to total residential sales

T = time

u = a disturbance term

P_R = average real price of electricity

X = the consumer price index

areas. To evaluate the net effect on distribution costs of population density, the percent of population living in rural areas is included in the price equation.

Transmission and distribution costs per kilowatt-hour sold are much lower for industrial customers than for residential customers. The lower average costs of utilities with a large share of sales to industrial customers, other things equal, may affect the price of electricity to residential customers because of the existence of joint costs or because of cross-subsidization between different types of services. Therefore, the ratio of total industrial sales to total residential sales is included in the price equation and is expected to have a negative sign.

A utility's cost curves may shift over time as a result of changes in technical efficiency or because of time-related cost elements that are not included explicitly in the price equation. A time-trend variable is included in the price equation to measure the direction and extent of the net effect on price of omitted time-related variables.

The price variable of relevance for the demand equation is real price, i.e., money price divided by the consumer price index. However, the rate-setting process is more likely to deal with nominal prices and costs. Therefore, the price equation is expressed in nominal terms and the following identity is included in the model:

$$P_R = N_R/X \tag{4.1}$$

where N_R is nominal price, and X is the consumer price index.

Data sources for the price, average consumption, and rural population variables are discussed in Chapter 3. Average hourly earnings in manufacturing data are from U.S. Bureau of the Census (various). Edison Electric Institute (various) data are used to calculate fuel cost as fuel costs per kilowatt-hour of nonhydroelectric generation times the percent of generation from nonhydroelectric sources. Where all generation is from hydroelectric sources, a value of 0.001 is used for the fuel cost variable so that all logs will exist. Data for the calculation of the percent of generation produced by public-owned utilities and the ratio of total industrial sales to total residential sales are also from Edison Electric Institute (various). Data on the consumer price index are from the U.S. Department of Commerce (various).

The data included in the price equations are state averages. If a significant amount of electricity is imported by a state, the relevant data for most of the variables would be that for the state producing the electricity rather than for the state consuming it. However, this difficulty is not too serious because there are not large divergences between the total amount of electricity consumed in each state and the amount produced in each. Also, imports will generally be from nearby states with similar cost structures.

The structural price equation is estimated by two-stage least squares. In the first stage, the endogenous electricity sales variable is regressed on all the exogenous variables in the model. The exogenous variables included in the final form of the demand equation are discussed in Chapter 3. Briefly, they are income, gas price, heating degree days, July temperature, percent rural population, average size of households, and time.

Empirical Results: Price Equation

A number of functional forms of the static price equation were estimated and compared on the basis of goodness of fit and plausibility of the results. The performance of the log-linear form was superior, and only these results are reported here.[2]

Parameter estimates obtained with the pooled sample are shown in Table 4-2.[3] The estimated coefficients of the quantity purchased, percent public-owned, and industrial sales variables are negative, as expected, and are highly significant. The estimated coefficients of the labor and fuel cost variables are positive, as expected, and highly significant; but the magnitude of the fuel cost coefficient is surprisingly small. The signs of the coefficients of percent rural population and time are both positive. The coefficient of the time variable is not statistically significant.

Beta coefficients for the price equation are shown in Table 4-3. Quantity purchased is by far the most important source of variation in price across observations. The second most important variable is the ratio of industrial to residential sales.

Table 4-2
Estimates of Parameters of the Residential Price Equation:
Pooled Sample[a]

Parameter	Estimate	Standard Error	Significance Level[b]
β_N	1.421	0.072	.0001
β_Q	−0.600	0.034	.0001
β_L	0.241	0.036	.0001
β_K	−0.018	0.004	.0001
β_F	0.011	0.003	.0002
β_U	0.028	0.013	.0313
β_I	−0.117	0.008	.0001
β_T	0.004	0.003	.1824
R^2 = 0.877			

[a]The number of observations is 432.
[b]Significance level for a two-tailed test based on the normal distribution. A significance level of .0001 indicates that the estimated parameter is significant at this level or above.

Table 4–3
Beta Coefficients for the Residential Price Equation

Variable	Beta Coefficient
Q_R	−0.777
L	0.166
K	−0.109
F	0.088
U	0.050
I	−0.258
T	0.040

The parameter estimates obtained with cross-section data for individual years are shown in Table 4-4. The estimated parameters are similar across years, and an analysis of covariance confirms the apparent constancy of the parameters over time. The value of the test statistic is 0.08, compared to the critical value for significance at the 10 percent level of 1.24. Thus pooling of the data for different years is appropriate.

In order to evaluate the robustness of the estimated parameters, the results obtained with the static model are compared to those for dynamic models. The response of the price schedule to changes in costs will not be instantaneous because of regulatory lags. However, there will be no lag in the response of price to quantity purchased, since the quantity purchased merely determines the customer's position on the price schedule. Therefore, the current value of quantity purchased is used in all dynamic equations.

Price equations involving simple lags in the explanatory variables are shown in Table 4-5, together with the estimated static equation for 1969. The results for distributed-lag models are shown in Table 4-6. The range of estimates of the coefficient of quantity purchased is −0.52 to −0.58 for the dynamic price equations, compared to −0.60 for the static equation estimated with pooled data. Thus the use of a static model appears to result in an underestimate of this coefficient, but the differences are not large relative to the estimated standard errors.

The range of dynamic estimates of the coefficient of wage costs, 0.14 to 0.20, is somewhat lower than the static estimate of 0.24, but the differences are not large relative to the estimated standard errors. The range for the coefficient of fuel costs is 0.01 to 0.02, compared to an estimate of 0.01 for the static model. The dynamic estimates of the remaining parameters are very similar to the static estimates.

Comparison of the static and dynamic results indicates that the estimated parameters of the price equation are very robust. Therefore, the estimates

Table 4-4
Estimates of Parameters of the Residential Price Equation: Individual Cross-Sections[a]

Year	β_N	β_Q	β_L	β_K	β_F	β_U	β_I	R^2
1961	1.405	-0.573	0.216	-0.103	0.017	0.016	0.023	0.865
1962	1.335	-0.565	0.257	-0.120	0.018	-0.018	0.034	0.877
1963	1.304	-0.576	0.292	-0.126	0.015	-0.022	0.038	0.883
1964	1.343	-0.608	0.300	-0.124	0.013	-0.018	0.043	0.895
1965	1.408	-0.624	0.274	-0.125	0.010	-0.018	0.039	0.890
1966	1.568	-0.632	0.213	-0.124	0.002	-0.019	0.019	0.879
1967	1.484	-0.603	0.239	-0.119	0.012	-0.017	0.018	0.879
1968	1.617	-0.602	0.162	-0.113	0.004	-0.018	0.010	0.866
1969	1.640	-0.591	0.128	-0.099	0.008	-0.014	0.014	0.859

Parameter

[a] The number of observations for each cross-section is 48.

Table 4-5
Residential Price Equation with Lagged Explanatory Variables[a]

Periods Lagged[b]	Parameter							
	β_N	β_Q	β_L	β_K	β_F	β_U	β_I	R^2
0	1.640[c]	−0.591[c]	0.128	−0.014	0.008	0.014	−0.099[c]	0.859
	(0.280)	(0.086)	(0.127)	(0.010)	(0.008)	(0.038)	(0.027)	
1	1.608[c]	−0.575[c]	0.138	−0.017	0.007	0.013	−0.104[c]	0.855
	(0.281)	(0.089)	(0.126)	(0.010)	(0.008)	(0.039)	(0.029)	
2	1.428[c]	−0.531[c]	0.201	−0.015	0.019[c]	0.020	−0.102[c]	0.871
	(0.279)	(0.087)	(0.117)	(0.010)	(0.008)	(0.036)	(0.027)	
Mixed	1.446[c]	−0.534[c]	0.203	−0.013	0.019[c]	0.023	−0.101[c]	0.871
	(0.272)	(0.087)	(0.111)	(0.010)	(0.008)	(0.035)	(0.027)	

[a]Figures in parentheses are asymptotic standard errors.
[b]Q is not lagged. All other variables are lagged the number of periods indicated. In the mixed equation, W is lagged five periods, I and F are lagged two periods, and the other variables are not lagged.
[c]Significant at the .05 level.

43

Table 4-6
Residential Price Equation with Distributed Lags[a]

Equation[b]		Parameter						
	β_N	β_Q	β_L	β_K	β_F	β_U	β_I	R^2
1st Order Pascal, $\lambda = 0.8$	1.487c (0.286)	−0.546c (0.088)	0.177 (0.120)	−0.017 (0.010)	0.017c (0.009)	0.018 (0.038)	−0.104c (0.027)	0.863
1st Order Pascal, $\lambda = 0.4$	1.593c (0.283)	−0.577c (0.087)	0.142 (0.126)	−0.015 (0.010)	0.010 (0.009)	0.015 (0.038)	−0.102c (0.028)	0.859
2nd Order Pascal, $\lambda = 0.8$	1.447c (0.283)	−0.525c (0.090)	0.188 (0.114)	−0.018 (0.011)	0.021c (0.009)	0.015 (0.038)	−0.104c (0.026)	0.866
2nd Order Pascal, $\lambda = 0.4$	1.546c (0.285)	−0.564c (0.087)	0.158 (0.124)	−0.016 (0.010)	0.013 (0.009)	0.017 (0.038)	−0.103c (0.028)	0.860
5-Year Invert. V	1.493c (0.286)	−0.551c (0.088)	0.175 (0.120)	−0.016 (0.010)	0.011 (0.009)	0.019 (0.038)	−0.103c (0.027)	0.862
9-Year Invert. V	1.442c (0.282)	−0.527c (0.090)	0.192 (0.114)	−0.018 (0.011)	0.021c (0.009)	0.017 (0.038)	−0.104 (0.026)	0.868
5-Year Simp. Av.	1.502c (0.286)	−0.553c (0.088)	0.172 (0.121)	−0.016 (0.010)	0.016 (0.009)	0.019 (0.038)	−0.103c (0.027)	0.862
9-Year Simp. Av.	1.453c (0.284)	−0.526c (0.090)	0.185 (0.115)	−0.018 (0.108)	0.020c (0.010)	0.015 (0.038)	−0.105c (0.027)	0.865

[a]Figures in parentheses are asymptotic standard errors.
[b]The number of observations for each equation is 48.
[c]Significant at the .05 level.

obtained with a static model can be considered to be reliable measures of the long-run response of electricity price to the explanatory variables.

In order to evaluate differences in the determinants of electricity price across geographic areas, separate static price equations are estimated for each of four areas. The estimated parameters are shown in Table 4-7. The estimated coefficients of quantity purchased are highly significant for all four areas. The estimates for the South and West are similar to the national estimate, while the estimates for the East and North are considerably larger in absolute magnitude.

The estimated coefficients of the wage-cost variable are significant for all four areas, but the estimate for the West has an incorrect sign. The coefficients of the variables for public ownership and industrial sales are significant only for the East and North. Fuel costs are significant only for the South and West. The estimated coefficients of fuel costs for the South and West are much larger than the national estimate.

Derivation of the Reduced-Form Equation

The total response of quantity purchased to changes in the explanatory variables will include indirect effects caused by the dependence of price on quantity purchased. In order to calculate estimates of the total elasticities of demand, it is necessary to obtain estimates of the parameters of the reduced-form equation for quantity purchased.

As discussed in Chapter 2, the reduced-form equation can either be derived from the estimated structural equations or estimated directly. This section discusses the reduced-form equation derived from the structural equations, and the next section discusses the results obtained by direct estimation.

Derivation of the reduced-form equation for quantity purchased from the structural equations is accomplished by substituting for the electricity price variable in the structural demand equation, equation (3.3), from the structural price equation, Table 4-2. The dependent variable in the price equation is nominal price. The equation can be expressed in real terms by subtracting the logarithm of the consumer price index from the right-hand side of the equation.

Substituting in the demand equation for P_R and solving for Q_R, the reduced-form equation is

$$\ln Q_R = -7.164 + 1.651 \ln Y + 0.130 \ln G_R - 0.077 \ln D$$
$$+ 1.734 \ln J + 0.794 \ln U - 0.775 \ln H - 0.890 \ln L + 0.434 \ln I$$
$$- 0.004 \ln F + 0.065 \ln K - 3.219 \ln X - 0.049T \quad (4.2)$$

The coefficients of Y, G_R, D, J, and H are equal to the estimated total elasticities of demand with respect to these variables. The variable for percent

Table 4-7
Residential Price Equation: Disaggregation by Geographic Area[a]

Parameter	East[b]	South[c]	North[d]	West[e]
β_N	1.666[f] (0.086)	−0.645 (0.582)	1.004[f] (0.144)	1.686[f] (0.196)
β_Q	−0.901[f] (0.101)	−0.510[f] (0.112)	−0.971[f] (0.074)	−0.632[f] (0.040)
β_L	0.292[f] (0.121)	0.336[f] (0.160)	0.646[f] (0.136)	−0.315[f] (0.153)
β_K	−0.011[f] (0.004)	−0.002 (0.010)	−0.026[f] (0.010)	0.013 (0.018)
β_F	0.002 (0.014)	0.550[f] (0.089)	0.010 (0.009)	0.016[f] (0.003)
β_U	0.066[f] (0.025)	0.065 (0.057)	0.194[f] (0.042)	0.101[f] (0.030)
β_I	−0.093[f] (0.019)	0.032 (0.045)	−0.158[f] (0.020)	0.001 (0.021)
β_T	0.018[f] (0.002)	−0.008 (0.012)	0.008 (0.005)	0.026[f] (0.005)
R^2	0.897	0.906	0.938	0.963
No. of Observations	126	108	63	99

[a]Figures in parentheses are estimated standard errors.
[b]New England, Middle Atlantic, and East North Central regions.
[c]South Atlantic and East South Central regions.
[d]West North Central region.
[e]Mountain and Pacific regions.
[f]Significant at the .05 level.

rural population, U, is included in both the demand and price equations. Therefore a change in U directly affects the price of electricity as well as the quantity purchased. The reduced-form coefficient of U measures the sum of the total effects on demand of both direct effects. The coefficients of L, I, F, K, and X measure the total effects on demand of changes in price caused by changes in these variables.

The demand equation can be written

$$\ln Q_R = a + b \ln P_R$$

where all other variables are omitted for simplicity. Similarly, the price equation can be written as

$$\ln P_R = d + e \ln Q_R$$

Then the effect on demand of a parallel shift in the price schedule would be equal to $b/(1 - be)$ times the shift. For the estimated coefficients in equation (3.3) and Table 4-2, the size of this multiplier is 3.219. Since changes in the general price level result in parallel shifts in the real price schedule, the coefficient of X is also 3.219 in equation (4.2).

Direct Estimation of the Reduced-Form Equation

The reduced-form equation can be directly estimated by using typical electric bill (TEB) data to construct an exogenous variable that represents the location and shape of the price schedule. Estimation by ordinary least squares of a demand equation that includes the TEB variable in place of average price provides consistent estimates of the reduced-form coefficients.

The main difficulty with this method lies in the construction of an appropriate TEB variable. As discussed in Chapter 2, the TEB data are not necessarily adequate indices of the price of various levels of consumption. Even if they were, the problem would remain of finding a combination of the data to represent the whole price schedule. Reduced-form equations are estimated for the pooled sample using data for the 250 kWh bill, the 500 kWh bill, the average of the two, and their difference.[4] The best results are obtained with data for the 250 kWh bill, and only these results are reported.

The estimated parameters of the static reduced-form equation for the pooled sample are shown in Table 4-8. The value of the R^2 is much lower for the reduced-form equation than for the structural demand equation. This is not surprising, given the inability of a single TEB variable to accurately represent the location and shape of the whole price schedule.

The estimated coefficient of the TEB variable measures the total response of demand to a change in the location or shape of the price schedule. If the shapes of the price schedules were constant, the TEB elasticity would measure the effect on demand of a parallel shift in the price schedule. However, the shapes of the price schedule cannot be assumed to be constant; and therefore, this elasticity is not directly comparable to the estimate derived from the structural equations.

The estimated coefficients of the other variables are equal to estimated total elasticities of demand. The total elasticities of demand should be larger in absolute magnitude than the direct elasticities. Comparison of the estimated coefficients in Table 4-8 with the estimated coefficients of the structural demand equation in equation (3.3) shows that this condition is satisfied for all variables except July temperature and time.

An analysis of covariance indicates that the parameters of the reduced-form equation, and thus the total elasticities of demand, are constant over time. The value of the test statistic is 0.30, compared to the critical value for significance at the 10 percent level of 1.24.

Table 4-8
Estimates of Parameters of the Residential Reduced-Form Equation:
Pooled Sample[a]

Variable[b]	Estimated Coefficient	Standard Error	Significance Level[c]
C	9.416	0.923	.0001
B_R	−1.526	0.070	.0001
Y	0.718	0.103	.0001
G_R	0.133	0.025	.0001
D	−0.147	0.028	.0001
J	0.346	0.191	.070
U	0.368	0.036	.0001
H	−0.273	0.204	.181
T	−0.004	0.005	.378
R^2 = 0.717			

[a]The number of observations is 432.
[b]C is the intercept, B is the TEB variable, and all other variables are defined in Table 3-1.
[c]Significance level for a two-tailed test based on the normal distribution. A significance level of .0001 indicates that the estimated coefficient is significant at this level or above.

Results obtained for dynamic reduced-form equations indicate that the estimated parameters are not very sensitive to the dynamic assumptions made. The range of estimates obtained for the coefficient of the TEB variable is −1.42 to −1.48, compared to an estimate of −1.53 for the static model. The differences are not large relative to the estimated standard errors. The range of estimates for the coefficient of income is 0.45 to 0.74 and thus brackets the static estimate of 0.72. The range for the estimated coefficient of gas price, 0.15 to 0.19, is somewhat higher than the static estimate of 0.13, but the differences are not large relative to the estimated standard errors.

Total Elasticities of Demand and Expenditure

Estimates of the total elasticities of demand have been obtained both by directly estimating the reduced-form equation using a TEB variable and by solving the estimated structural demand and price equations for quantity purchased. The estimates obtained using the two methods are quite dissimilar. The estimate of the total income elasticity of demand derived from the structural equations is 1.65, while the direct estimate is 0.72. The estimates of the elasticities of demand with respect to July temperature, percent rural population, and household size are also larger in absolute magnitude when derived from the structural equations than when estimated directly (see equation (4.2) and Table 4-8).

The sensitivity of the estimates to the method used to obtain them is unfortunate because the total elasticities have considerable potential interest for policy purposes. For example, the total income elasticity of demand determines the distributional effect of a unit tax on residential purchases of electricity. Such a tax would be progressive if the total income elasticity of demand were greater than one and regressive if it were less than one. Since the estimate of the total income elasticity is greater than one when derived from the structural equations and less than one when estimated directly, it is not clear what the distributional effect of a unit tax would be.

The distributional effect of an *ad valorem* tax on residential purchases of electricity is determined by the total income elasticity of expenditure on electricity. Because price is a function of quantity purchased, the total income elasticity of expenditure is not equal to the total income elasticity of demand. The formula for the expenditure elasticity is

$$E_x = E_y(1 + E_q)$$

where E_x is the total income elasticity of expenditure, E_y is the total income elasticity of demand, and E_q is the direct elasticity of price with respect to quantity purchased. The estimate of the total income elasticity of expenditure is 0.66 if derived from the structural equations and 0.28 if directly estimated using a TEB variable. Thus the results do indicate that an *ad valorem* tax on residential purchases of electricity would be regressive.[5]

Notes

1. The reduced-form equation can also be estimated by including in the equation for quantity purchased all the exogenous variables appearing in the price equation. The estimates of the total elasticities using this approach are similar to those obtained with a typical electric bill (TEB) variable.

2. Results for other functional forms are discussed in Halvorsen (1972).

3. The results shown are for the model in which the appliance price and housing structure variables are omitted from the demand equation.

4. The typical electric bill (TEB) data are from U.S. Federal Power Commission (various). The data are reported as of January 1 of each year. To approximate the average values for each year, beginning and end of year TEB data are averaged. Data on the 500 kWh bill are not available for January 1, 1961. Therefore, data for January 1, 1962 are used as proxies for the average values for 1961.

5. The 1962 *Survey of Consumer Expenditure* provided data on expenditures on electricity by income level. The average expenditure on electricity was $40.15 for families with incomes of $1,000 to $2,000, and $128.15 for those with incomes of $10,000 to $14,000. The implied income elasticity of expenditure is 0.31.

Appendix 4A
Reduced-Form Equation
for Cities

Introduction

The estimated elasticities of demand discussed in Chapters 3 and 4 are obtained using state data. The use of data for cities would provide larger sample sizes and would involve a lower degree of aggregation. Unfortunately, data on average electricity price are not available by city, and therefore the structural demand equation cannot be estimated using city data. However, TEB data are available by city, making it possible to estimate the reduced-form equation for quantity purchased.

This appendix discusses the estimates of total elasticities of demand obtained for cities using TEB data. The estimated coefficient of the TEB variable is highly significant but somewhat smaller in absolute magnitude than the estimate for states. The estimated total income elasticity of demand for cities is not significant, apparently because of errors of measurement and specification. The estimated total elasticity of demand with respect to gas price is somewhat larger for cities than for states.

Specification of the Reduced-Form Equation

The reduced-form equation for quantity puchased includes the variables that would be included in a structural demand equation, as well as a TEB variable representing the exogenous variables that would be included in a structural price equation. Data limitations result in some differences in the specification of the reduced-form equation for city data and that for states. Table 4A–1 summarizes the specification of the reduced-form equation estimated with city data.

The income variable included in the equation is median family income. Average per capita income is a better index of the standard of living because it is not affected by family size, but data on average per capita income are not available for cities.

Data on average gas price are for the gas utility serving each city. Since the utilities' marketing areas are not in general coterminous with city limits, the gas price variable will contain potentially serious errors of measurement.

Average December temperature is used to measure heating requirements because data for it are available for more cities than are data for heating degree days. Average July temperature is again used as the measure of cooling requirements.

51

Table 4A-1

Specification of the Residential Reduced-Form Equation: City Data

$$\ln Q_R = \gamma_Q + \gamma_B \ln B_R + \gamma_Y \ln Y + \gamma_G \ln G_R + \gamma_D \ln D + \gamma_J \ln J$$
$$+ \gamma_U \ln U + \gamma_M \ln M + \gamma_T T + u$$

where Q_R = average annual residential electricity sales per customer, in thousands of kWh

B_R = average of typical electric bills for 250 kWh and 500 kWh deflated by the consumer price index, in dollars

Y = median family income, in thousands of dollars

G_R = average real price of gas, in cents per therm

D = average December temperature, in degrees Fahrenheit

J = average July temperature, in degrees Fahrenheit

U = size of city, measured as total population divided by 100,000

M = population density per square mile

T = time

u = a disturbance term

By definition, the percent of population living in rural areas is zero for all cities. However, differences in demand resulting from factors similar to those discussed for rural and nonrural customers may exist between small cities and large cities. Therefore, city population is included in the equation and is expected to have a negative coefficient. The relative importance of different types of housing can also be expected to affect the average consumption of electricity in a city. Since the composition of the housing stock is reflected in the population density of the city, population per square mile is included in the equation and is expected to have a negative coefficient.

TEB data are available for 250 kWh and 500 kWh consumption levels for the full period. Beginning and end of year data are averaged for each year. Reduced-form equations are estimated with data for the 250 kWh bill, the 500 kWh bill, their average, and their difference. The best results are obtained using the average of the two bills, and only these results are reported.

Data on typical electric bills and on average sales per customer are from U.S. Federal Power Commission (various). Data by city on 1959 median family income are available in U.S. Bureau of the Census (1962). To obtain income data by city for the years 1961 through 1969, the 1959 median family income data are multiplied by indices of average per capita income by state from U.S. Department of Commerce (various). The assumption that year-to-year changes in median family income are proportional to changes in state average per capita income will clearly result in errors of measurement in the income variable.

Gas price data are from *Brown's Directory* (various). The average price per thousand cubic feet and the Btu content of the gas are available. From this data the price per therm is calculated. The gas price, income, and TEB data are all deflated by the consumer price index.

Data on average December temperature, average July temperature, size of city, and population density are from U.S. Bureau of the Census (1962). The temperature data are averages for the period 1931-1960. The data on city size and population density are for 1960. Since neither variable will change rapidly over time, use of 1960 data should not introduce serious measurement errors.

The sample includes data for 229 cities for the years 1961 through 1969. Thus 2061 observations are available. The only criterion for the inclusion or exclusion of a city from the sample is the availability of adequate data. Because data are generally available only for cities with 25,000 or more residents, very small cities are not included in the sample.

Empirical Results

The performance of the log-linear reduced-form equation is superior to that of other functional forms, and only the log-linear results are reported here. The estimated parameters of the reduced-form equation obtained using the pooled sample are shown in Table 4A-2. The fit of the city reduced-form equation is inferior to that for states. The R^2 for the city equation is 0.61, compared to 0.72 for the state equation (see Table 4-8).

The estimated coefficient of the TEB variable is highly significant but somewhat smaller in absolute magnitude than the estimate obtained using state data. The difference between state and city data with respect to the estimated coefficient of income is striking. The estimate of this coefficient, and thus of the total income elasticity of demand, is 0.72 for state data but only 0.05, and not significant, for city data.

While it is possible that the total income elasticity of demand actually is very small for cities, it seems more plausible that the low estimate for cities is due to errors of measurement and specification. The income variable can be expected to contain large measurement errors because of violations of the assumption that year-to-year changes in city median family income are proportional to changes in state average per capita income. The probability of specification error arises as a result of the omission of a variable for household size. This variable could not be included in the city reduced-form equation because of lack of data. Since household size appears to have a negative effect on electricity consumption, and can be expected to be positively correlated with median family income, the omission of household size should cause a downward bias in the estimated coefficient of median family income.

Table 4A-2
Estimates of Parameters of the Residential Reduced-Form Equation:
City Data[a]

Variable[b]	Estimated Coefficient	Standard Error	Significance Level[c]
C	−3.946	0.441	.0001
B	−1.364	0.037	.0001
Y	0.052	0.040	.199
G	0.242	0.018	.0001
D	−0.013	0.016	.422
J	1.877	0.095	.0001
U	−0.034	0.006	.0001
M	−0.171	0.010	.0001
T	0.026	0.003	.0001
R^2 = 0.608			

[a]The number of observations is 2061.
[b]C is the intercept. All other variables are defined in Table 4A-1.
[c]Significance level for a two-tailed test based on the normal distribution. A significance level of .0001 indicates that the estimated coefficient is significant at this level or above.

The estimated total elasticity of demand with respect to gas price is 0.24 for cities, compared to 0.13 for states. The estimated coefficient of July temperature is also larger for cities than for states. The estimated coefficients of city size and population density are both highly significant and have the expected negative signs.

The coefficient of the time variable is positive and highly significant. The reduced-form coefficient of time reflects shifts in both the demand and price schedules. Therefore, its positive sign does not necessarily indicate that the demand equation has shifted upward over time for customers living in cities.

An analysis of covariance indicates that the parameters of the reduced-form equation, and thus the total elasticities of demand, are constant over time. The value of the test statistic is 0.37, compared to the critical value for significance at the 10 percent level of 1.24.

In order to test the validity of the static equation coefficients as measures of long-run total elasticities, various dynamic formulations of the reduced-form equation are estimated. The results indicate that the estimated elasticities are not very sensitive to the dynamic assumptions made. The range of dynamic estimates of the coefficient of the TEB variable is −1.24 to −1.33, compared to −1.36 for the static model. The estimates of the total income elasticity of demand are insignificant for the dynamic equations as well as for the static equation. The range of the dynamic estimates of the total elasticity of demand with respect to gas price is 0.24 to 0.30, compared to the static estimate of 0.24

5

Commercial and Industrial Electricity Demand

Introduction

Sales to the commercial and industrial sectors account for approximately two-thirds of total electricity consumption in the United States. Despite their importance, these sectors have received less attention in the electricity demand literature than has the residential sector. In this chapter, models of electricity demand are estimated for both sectors. The results indicate that the direct long-run elasticity of demand with respect to electricity price is approximately unitary in the commercial sector and is substantially greater than unity in absolute magnitude in the industrial sector.

Specification of the Electricity Price Equations

Two alternative specifications of the price equation are estimated. In one specification, cost variables are used to explain the shape and location of the price schedule. In the alternative specification, typical electric bill (TEB) variables are used as direct measures of the price schedule. Both specifications are summarized in Table 5-1.

The specification incorporating cost variables is similar to that for the residential price equation. The equation includes variables for fuel, labor, and capital costs, factors affecting transmission and distribution costs, and the composition of sales. One difference between the specification used here and the specification for the residential sector is that fuel costs are represented by two variables, the cost of fuel per kilowatt-hour from nonhydroelectric generation and the percent of generation from nonhydroelectric sources. In the residential equation these two variables are combined into one variable, the cost of fuel per kilowatt-hour of total generation. Another difference is that the composition of sales is measured by the inclusion of total sales to each sector, while in the residential equation only the ratio of industrial to residential sales is included. The sectoral sales variables are treated as endogenous variables in the estimation procedure.

The alternative specification incorporating TEB variables cannot provide information on the effects of costs on electricity price. However, it does satisfy the requirements for identification and consistent estimation of the parameters of the demand equation.

Table 5-1
Specification of the Commercial and Industrial Price Equations

Equation with Cost Variables:

$$\ln P_i = \alpha_P + \alpha_Q \ln Q_{ia} + \alpha_F \ln F + \alpha_S \ln S + \alpha_L \ln L + \alpha_K \ln K + \alpha_Z \ln Z$$
$$+ \alpha_U \ln U + \alpha_R \ln Q_R + \alpha_C \ln Q_C + \alpha_I \ln Q_I + u$$

Equation with Typical Electric Bill (TEB) Variables:

$$\ln P_i = \gamma_P + \gamma_Q \ln Q_{ia} + \gamma_1 \ln B_{i1} + \gamma_2 \ln B_{i2} + \gamma_3 \ln B_{i3} + u$$

where

P_i = average price of electricity per kilowatt-hour in sector i, $i = C, I$

Q_{ia} = average purchase of electricity per customer in sector i, $i = C, I$

F = cost of fuel per kilowatt-hour from nonhydroelectric generation

S = percent of total generation from nonhydroelectric sources

L = index of the cost of labor

K = sales of public-owned utilities as percent of total sales

Z = population per square mile

U = percent rural population

Q_R, Q_C, Q_I = total purchases of electric energy by the residential, commercial, and industrial sectors

B_{i1}, B_{i2}, B_{i3} = typical electric bills for first three levels of consumption in sector i, $i = C, I$

u = a disturbance term.

Specification of the Commercial Electricity Demand Equation

Commercial demand for electricity is assumed to be a function of the level of output in the commercial sector, the prices of electricity and gas, the cost of labor, income, and several noneconomic variables. The level of output in the commercial sector is in turn assumed to be a function of population size, the prices of electricity and gas, the cost of labor, income, and noneconomic variables. Because adequate data are not available on the level of output of the commercial sector, this variable is eliminated by substitution in the demand equation, as discussed below. The specification of the final demand equation is summarized in Table 5-2.

The basic demand equation is

$$\ln Q_C = a_0 + a_1 \ln V_C + a_2 \ln P_C + a_3 \ln G_C + a_4 \ln L_C + a_5 \ln Y$$
$$+ a_6 \ln J + a_7 \ln D + a_8 \ln Z + a_9 \ln U + v \quad (5.1)$$

Table 5-2
Specification of the Commercial and Industrial Demand Equations

Commercial Sector

Quantity purchased:

$$\ln Q_C = \alpha_Q + \alpha_N \ln N + \alpha_E \ln P_C + \alpha_G \ln G_C + \alpha_L \ln L_C + \alpha_Y \ln Y$$
$$+ \alpha_J \ln J + \alpha_D \ln D + \alpha_Z \ln Z + \alpha_U \ln U + \alpha_H \ln H + u$$

Industrial Sector

Quantity purchased:

$$\ln Q_I = \beta_Q + \beta_M \ln V_M + \beta_A \ln V_A + \beta_E \ln P_I + \beta_G \ln G_I + \beta_L \ln L_I$$
$$+ \beta_J \ln J + \beta_D \ln D + u$$

Value added in manufacturing:

$$\ln V_I = \gamma_V + \gamma_N \ln N + \gamma_E \ln P_I + \gamma_Y \ln Y + \gamma_G \ln G_I + \gamma_L \ln L_I + \gamma_Z \ln Z + u$$

where

Q_i = total purchases of electricity by sector i, $i = C, I$

P_i = average price of electricity to sector i, $i = C, I$

G_i = average price per therm for all types of gas purchased by sector i, $i = C, I$

Y = per capita personal income

J = average July temperature

D = heating degree days

Z = population per square mile

U = percent rural population

H = percent of housing units in single-unit structures

N = population size

L_i = index of cost of labor to sector i, $I = C, I$

V_M = value added in manufacturing

V_A = value of mineral production

u = a disturbance term

where V_C is the level of output of the commercial sector, v is a disturbance term, and all other variables are defined in Table 5-2. The equation for V_C is,

$$\ln V_C = c_0 + c_1 \ln N + c_2 \ln P_C + c_3 \ln G_C + c_4 \ln L_C + c_5 \ln Y$$
$$+ c_6 \ln Z + c_7 \ln U + c_8 \ln H + w \quad (5.2)$$

where w is a disturbance term.[1]

Substitution for V_C in equation (5.1) from equation (5.2) yields the final demand equation:

$$\ln Q_C = a_0 + a_1 c_0 + a_1 c_1 \ln N + (a_2 + a_1 c_2) \ln P_C + (a_3 + a_1 c_3) \ln G_C$$
$$+ (a_4 + a_1 c_4) \ln L_C + (a_5 + a_1 c_5) \ln Y + a_6 \ln J + a_7 \ln D$$
$$+ (a_8 + a_1 c_6) \ln Z + (a_9 + a_1 c_7) \ln U + c_8 \ln H + v + a_1 w \quad (5.3)$$

which has the same form as the demand equation shown in Table 5-2.

The level of output of the commercial sector will have a positive effect on commercial demand for electricity, so a_1 will be positive. Since population can be expected to have a positive effect on the level of output in the commercial sector, c_1 should be positive. Given positive signs for a_1 and c_1, the coefficient of population in the final demand equation, which is equal to $a_1 c_1$, should be positive.

The price of electricity should have a negative effect on the level of output in the commerical sector and should also have a negative effect on the amount of electricity purchased per unit of output. Therefore a_2 and c_2 can be expected to be negative, and the coefficient of electricity price in the final demand equation, which is equal to $a_2 + a_1 c_2$, should be negative.

Income should have a positive effect on the level of output in the commercial sector and can be expected to have a positive effect on purchases of electricity per unit of output as a result of a positive income elasticity of demand for air conditioning, better lighting, etc. Since a_1, a_5, and c_5 should be positive, the coefficient of income in the final demand equation can be expected to be positive.

The price of gas can be expected to have a positive effect on the demand for electricity per unit of output but a negative effect on the level of output. Since a_3 should be positive and c_3 should be negative, the coefficient of gas price in the final demand equation, which is equal to $a_3 + a_1 c_3$, cannot be determined a priori. Labor may be either a complement or a substitute for electricity; so the sign of a_4 may be either negative or positive, and the sign of the coefficient of labor cost in the final demand equation also cannot be determined a priori.

The coefficients of average July temperature and heating degree days will reflect respectively the effect of greater cooling and heating requirements on the demand for electricity per unit of output. For reasons analogous to those discussed in Chapter 3 for the residential sector, the coefficient of July temperature should be positive and the coefficient of heating degree days cannot be determined a priori. The percent of housing units in single-unit structures can be expected to have a negative effect on the level of output in the commercial sector and therefore should have a negative effect on commercial electricity demand.

The geographic distribution of population should affect both the level of output in the commercial sector and the use of electricity per unit of output. Since the level of output should be positively affected by population density, the coefficient of population per square mile in equation (5.2) should be positive and the coefficient of percent rural population should be negative. However, the amount of electricity used per unit of output may be negatively affected by population density, because of the existence of economies of scale in the production of commercial services. Therefore, the sign of a_8 may be negative and the sign of a_9 may be positive. Since offsetting effects are involved for both variables, it is not clear what the signs of their coefficients should be.

Specification of the Industrial Electricity Demand Equation

The quantity of electricity purchased by the industrial sector is assumed to be a function of value added in manufacturing, minerals production, the prices of electricity and gas, labor costs, and climate.[2] The specification of the demand equation is summarized in Table 5-2. The coefficients of value added in manufacturing, minerals production, and gas price should be positive. The coefficient of July temperature can be expected to be positive, but the sign of the coefficient of heating degree days may be either positive or negative. The coefficient of labor costs could be either positive or negative, because labor could be either a substitute or complement for electricity.

The amount of manufacturing activity in a state will not be independent of the price of electricity because energy costs will affect the locational decisions of firms. Therefore, value added in manufacturing is treated as endogenous.[3] The equation for manufacturing value added shown in Table 5-2 can be interpreted as the reduced-form equation of a model incorporating demand and supply relationships. Since the level of manufacturing will be positively affected by market size, the coefficients of population size and per capita income are expected to be positive. The level of manufacturing output will be negatively affected by the prices of inputs, so the coefficients of the prices of electricity, gas, and labor should be negative. Since the costs of production should be negatively affected by population density, the coefficient of population per square mile can be expected to be positive.

A change in the price of electricity in a single state will affect demand for electricity both directly and through its effect on the locational decisions of firms. The own-price elasticity of demand for states will therefore be equal to $\beta_E + \beta_M \gamma_E$ where β_E and γ_E are the coefficients of electricity price in the equations for quantity purchased and value added, respectively, and β_M is the coefficient of value added in the equation for quantity purchased. However, this is not an appropriate measure of the response of demand to a nationwide price change, because a change affecting all states equally would not induce the same locational effects.[4]

The coefficient of price in the equation for quantity purchased, β_E, can be used as an estimate of the national price elasticity. This estimate involves two biases that are assumed to offset each other. A downward bias will exist because the level of manufacturing activity will not be completely independent of nationwide changes in the price of electric energy. And an upward bias will exist because the estimate of β_E will reflect the locational effects of cross-sectional differences in electricity price on the composition of manufacturing activity by state.

Data Sources

All equations are estimated with cross-section data for the 48 contiguous states for 1969. Data on average electricity price, total quantity purchased, quantity purchased per customer, cost of fuel, percent nonhydroelectric generation, and percent of sales by public-owned utilities are from Edison Electric Institute (various). Typical electric bill (TEB) data are from U.S. Federal Power Commission (various). Data for the 750, 1500, and 6000 kWh bills are used for the commercial sector, and data for the 30,000, 60,000, and 200,000 kWh bills are used for the industrial sector. Gas price data are from American Gas Association (various).

Data for average July temperature and heating degree days are weighted averages of city data in U.S. Bureau of the Census (1962). Data on the percent of housing units in single-unit structures are from U.S. Bureau of the Census (1970). Population size, percent rural population, value of mineral production, and population per square mile are from U.S. Bureau of the Census (various). Per capita income data are from U.S. Department of Commerce (various).

Data on average annual earnings in retail trade from U.S. Bureau of the Census (various) are used as an index of the cost of labor to the commercial sector. Data on average hourly earnings in industry 20, food and kindred products, are used as an index of the cost of labor to both the industrial sector and to electric utilities.[5] Data on earnings in industry 20, as well as on value added in manufacturing, are from U.S. Bureau of the Census (1969).

Empirical Results: Commercial Sector

The commercial demand equation is estimated for both the model in which the price equation incorporates cost variables, the Cost Model, and the model in which TEB variables are used to explain price, the TEB Model. Estimates of the parameters of the demand equation for the Cost and TEB Models are shown in the second and third columns respectively of Table 5-3. Since the demand equations are log-linear, the estimated parameters are equal to the estimated direct elasticities of demand.

All estimated parameters are similar for the two models except for the estimate of the own-price elasticity, α_E, which is much smaller in absolute magnitude for the TEB Model.[6] Since an examination of the residuals indicates

Table 5-3
Estimates of Parameters of the Commercial Demand Equations[a]

| Parameter[b] | Demand Equation with No Dummies | | Demand Equation with State Dummies | |
	Cost Model	TEB Model	Cost Model	TEB Model
α_Q	−0.907	−5.058	−0.806	−2.421
α_N	0.923[c] (0.043)	0.923[c] (0.044)	0.926[c] (0.029)	0.924[c] (0.029)
α_E	−1.157[c] (0.259)	−0.562[c] (0.218)	−1.208[c] (0.217)	−0.916[c] (0.155)
α_Y	1.376[c] (0.413)	1.154[c] (0.427)	1.306[c] (0.279)	1.249[c] (0.276)
α_G	−0.128 (0.133)	−0.127 (0.139)	−0.183[c] (0.092)	−0.193[c] (0.091)
α_L	−0.667 (0.790)	0.273 (0.784)	−0.694 (0.554)	−0.276 (0.507)
α_J	0.197 (0.617)	0.238 (0.644)	0.359 (0.422)	0.321 (0.419)
α_D	−0.175 (0.090)	−0.218[c] (0.093)	−0.176[c] (0.065)	−0.207[c] (0.062)
α_Z	−0.138[c] (0.038)	−0.144[c] (0.040)	−0.114[c] (0.026)	−0.116[c] (0.026)
α_U	−0.078 (0.118)	−0.144 (0.122)	−0.042 (0.080)	−0.052 (0.079)
α_H	−0.621 (0.387)	−0.136 (0.382)	−0.738[c] (0.272)	−0.526[c] (0.248)
D_1	−	−	−0.749[c] (0.149)	−0.640[c] (0.137)
D_2	−	−	0.432[c] (0.145)	0.520[c] (0.136)
$\overline{R}^2$	0.970	0.970	0.986	0.986

[a]Figures in parentheses are estimated standard errors. The number of observations is 48.
[b]D_1 and D_2 are the coefficients of the Tennessee and Utah dummy variables respectively.
[c]Significant at the .05 level.

that the observations for Tennessee and Utah are outliers, the demand equations are reestimated with dummy variables included for these states.

The parameter estimates obtained with the dummy variables included are shown in the fourth and fifth columns of Table 5-3. The inclusion of the dummy variables results in only small changes in most of the estimated parameters for both models.[7] However, the estimated own-price elasticity becomes much larger in absolute value for the TEB Model and more nearly equal to the other estimates of this elasticity. The second estimate for the TEB Model also coincides more closely with the plausible assumption that commercial demand is not significantly less elastic than residential demand. Therefore, it is reasonable to discount the one low estimate and to conclude that the own-price elasticity of demand in the commercial sector is approximately unitary.

The estimated coefficients of population, income, July temperature, and percent of housing units in single-unit structures have the expected signs. The signs of the coefficients of the other variables could not be determined a priori because they involved offsetting effects. For example, the negative sign of the coefficient of gas price is not inconsistent with the assumption that gas is a substitute for electricity, because gas price can be expected to have a negative effect on the level of output in the commercial sector.

The estimated parameters of the price equations are very similar for models including and excluding the state dummies. Only the results for the model excluding the dummy variables will be discussed here. The estimation results for the price equation incorporating cost variables are shown in Table 5-4. In general, the estimated coefficients of the cost variables have the expected signs but are insignificant. The performance of the price equation incorporating TEB variables is much better. As shown in Table 5-5, all parameter estimates are significant at the 5 percent level, and the value of R^2 is 0.87, compared to 0.54 for the equation incorporating cost variables.

Empirical Results: Industrial Sector

The estimated parameters of the equation for quantity purchased are shown in the second and third columns of Table 5-6 for the Cost and TEB Models respectively. The estimated own-price elasticity is highly significant and greater than unity in absolute magnitude for both models. The estimated coefficients of the manufacturing and mining output variables are positive and highly significant for both models. The cross-elasticity of demand with respect to gas price is positive, as expected, but is not significant at the 5 percent level using a two-tailed test. The estimated coefficient of labor cost is negative, indicating that labor may be a complement rather than a substitute for electricity, but the estimates are not significant at the 5 percent level.

Table 5–4
Estimates of Parameters of the Price Equations
Incorporating Cost Variables[a]

Parameter	Commercial Sector	Industrial Sector
α_P	0.902	1.313
α_Q	−0.377[b] (0.145)	−0.135 (0.070)
α_F	0.019 (0.168)	0.123 (0.317)
α_S	0.013 (0.009)	0.032 (0.012)
α_L	0.201 (0.162)	0.363 (0.208)
α_K	−0.022 (0.030)	−0.031 (0.042)
α_Z	0.051 (0.038)	0.125[b] (0.055)
α_U	0.088 (0.105)	0.292 (0.152)
α_R	−0.201 (0.192)	−0.174 (0.250)
α_C	0.328 (0.172)	0.419[b] (0.206)
α_I	−0.133 (0.084)	−0.297 (0.166)
$\overline{R}^2$	0.540	0.713

[a]Figures in parentheses are estimated standard errors. The number of observations is 48
[b]Significant at the .05 level.

Estimates of the parameters of the equation for value added in manufacturing are shown in the fourth and fifth columns of Table 5-6. The coefficient of electricity price has the expected negative sign and is significant at the 5 percent level for both models. The signs of the coefficients of income, gas price, and labor cost are opposite to those expected, but none of these coefficients are statistically significant. The coefficients of the population size and population density variables are significant and have the expected positive signs.

As discussed previously, an estimate of the national own-price elasticity for electricity is provided by the coefficient of electricity price in the equation for quantity purchased. The estimated value of this coefficient is significantly greater than unity in absolute magnitude for both models, indicating that industrial demand is elastic even on the national level. The own-price elasticity

Table 5-5
Estimates of Parameters of the Price Equations
Incorporating TEB Variables[a]

Parameter	Commercial Sector	Industrial Sector
γ_P	-4.270^{b}	-6.647^{b}
γ_Q	-0.207^{b} (0.046)	-0.117 (0.070)
γ_1	0.667^{b} (0.213)	-0.197 (0.805)
γ_2	-0.766^{b} (0.253)	0.699 (1.178)
γ_3	0.928^{b} (0.160)	0.774 (0.668)
$\overline{R}^2$	0.873	0.695

[a]Figures in parentheses are estimated standard errors. The number of observations is 48.
[b]Significant at the .05 level.

for individual states is higher than the national elasticity because it includes the effect of price on the level of manufacturing activity. Substituting for value added in manufacturing in the equation for quantity purchased from the equation for value added yields estimates of the state own-price elasticity of -1.75 and -1.53 for the Cost and TEB Models respectively.

The estimated parameters of the industrial price equation incorporating cost variables are shown in Table 5-4. The estimated coefficients all have the appropriate signs and are more frequently significant than for the corresponding equation for the commercial sector. While the price equation incorporating cost variables performs better than that for the commercial sector, the price equation incorporating TEB variables performs worse. As shown in Table 5-5, none of the TEB variables have significant coefficients in the industrial price equation.

Notes

1. Equation (5.2) is the reduced-form equation for an implicit model incorporating equations for the demand and supply of commercial services.

2. Fuel oil and coal are important substitutes for electric energy in the industrial sector, but their prices could not be included in the demand equation because of lack of data. Two sets of proxies were tried for these variables: prices calculated from data in the *Census of Manufacturing* for 1962 and the price paid by electric utilities in 1969. The results obtained when either set of proxies were

Table 5-6
Estimates of Parameters of the Industrial Demand Equations[a]

Variable[b]	Quantity Purchased		Value Added in Manufacturing	
	Cost Model	TEB Model	Cost Model	TEB Model
C	−3.493	−0.613	6.446	6.185
V_M	0.669[c] (0.039)	0.680[c] (0.040)	N/I	N/I
V_A	0.187[c] (0.036)	0.184[c] (0.037)	N/I	N/I
P_I	−1.404[c] (0.159)	−1.242[c] (0.177)	−0.520[c] (0.196)	−0.423[c] (0.212)
G_I	0.293 (0.161)	0.229 (0.164)	0.179 (0.179)	0.173 (0.178)
L_I	−0.393 (0.353)	−0.509 (0.361)	0.773 (0.447)	0.717 (0.447)
J	0.875 (0.875)	0.472 (0.908)	N/I	N/I
D	0.050 (0.121)	0.029 (0.125)	N/I	N/I
N	N/I	N/I	1.042[c] (0.079)	1.052[c] (0.079)
Y	N/I	N/I	−0.471 (0.491)	−0.450 (0.490)
Z	N/I	N/I	0.329[c] (0.071)	0.319[c] (0.071)
$\overline{R}^2$	0.954	0.952	0.939	0.940

[a]Figures in parentheses are estimated standard errors. The number of observations is 48.
[b]C is the intercept.
[c]Significant at the .05 level.
N/I means the variable is not included in this equation.

included in the demand equation were similar to those shown below for the equation omitting these variables.

    3. The level of mineral production can be treated as exogenous because it is determined primarily by the location of mineral deposits.

    4. It should be emphasized that the estimated own-price elasticity of demand for the commercial sector can be used to evaluate national as well as

state policies, because the location of commercial activities can be assumed to be independent of the price of electricity.

5. Industry 20 is chosen because average hourly earnings data are available for this industry for all states.

6. Results obtained using ordinary least squares are similar to those for the Cost Model for all variables, including electricity price. The estimated own-price elasticity is 0.944.

7. The estimated standard errors are generally smaller for the demand equation including dummy variables, and the number of parameter estimates significant at the five percent level increases.

Part II
Substitution among Types of Energy

6

Derivation of Energy Demand Models Using Duality Theory

Introduction

The number of applications of duality theory in economics has increased rapidly in recent years.[1] One of the principal advantages of duality theory is that it allows the derivation by simple differentiation of systems of demand equations that are consistent with maximizing or minimizing behavior on the part of an economic agent. The alternative procedure of explicitly solving a constrained maximization or minimization problem is computationally more cumbersome, and is generally not possible if flexible functional forms are used.[2]

By facilitating the use of flexible functional forms, duality theory makes it possible to obtain estimates of elasticities of demand and substitution that are subject to minimal a priori restrictions. In contrast, the nonflexible functional forms used in explicit solutions of maximization or minimization problems place severe restrictions on the estimated elasticities. For example, the CES functional form constrains all cross-elasticities of substitution to be constant and equal, and the Cobb-Douglas form imposes the additional restriction that they all equal unity.

Duality theory also provides alternative representations of the same technology. Therefore, a model can be chosen that yields demand equations with desirable properties for the particular problem at hand. As discussed in Diewert (1974) and Lau (1974*a*), the alternatives include production functions, profit functions, and cost functions.

The use of a normalized restricted profit function to derive a model of interfuel substitution in electric power generation is discussed in the next section. The derivation of a model of energy substitution in manufacturing using a unit cost function is discussed in the subsequent section.

Interfuel Substitution in Electric Power Generation

Electric utilities account for about two-thirds the coal, one-tenth the oil, and one-fifth the natural gas consumed as fuel in the United States.[3] Thus the extent of interfuel substitution in existing electric power plants is an important determinant of the short-run price responsiveness of aggregate energy demand. The model developed here makes it possible to estimate elasticities of demand

69

and substitution for fuels in existing plants. Other characteristics of the production process are also examined.

The quantity of electricity produced by an existing conventional steam electric power plant is assumed to be a function of variable fuel inputs and fixed capital and labor inputs:

$$E = E(Y, Z)$$

where E is electric energy and Y and Z are vectors of variable and fixed inputs respectively. The characteristics of interfuel substitution could be examined by direct estimation of the parameters of the production function. However, derivation of the model using duality theory offers both theoretical and statistical advantages. The use of a normalized restricted profit function provides the most suitable basis for study of electric power generation and is the approach used here.

The normalized restricted profit function dual to the production function can be written:

$$\Pi = \Pi(P, Z)$$

where Π is normalized restricted profit, P is a vector of the normalized prices of the variable inputs, and Z is a vector of the quantities of the fixed inputs. The specification of the normalized restricted profit function is

$$\Pi = \Pi(P_C, P_O, P_G, Z_K, Z_L, Z_T)$$

where P_C = the normalized price of coal

         P_O = the normalized price of oil

         P_G = the normalized price of gas

         Z_K = capital service input

         Z_L = labor input

         Z_T = the vintage of the capital

The prices of the variable inputs are normalized by dividing by the price of output.

One advantage of estimating a normalized restricted profit function is that the righthand-side variables can be considered exogenous since they consist of the prices of the variable inputs and the quantities of the fixed inputs. Another important advantage is that estimation of a normalized restricted profit function with capital as a fixed input avoids the necessity of explicitly modeling the effects of rate-of-return regulation on input choice. Profit maximization subject to a rate-of-return constraint may result in the use of more than the cost minimizing amount of capital relative to other inputs, the "Averch-Johnson effect," but will not distort interfuel substitution given fixed capital.[4]

Treating labor as a fixed input also avoids complications arising from rate-of-return regulation, as well as minimizing potential problems arising from the poor quality of available data on labor prices. The assumption that capital and labor are fixed inputs in existing plants is consistent with previous studies,[5] and is not critical for the use of a normalized restricted profit function. As discussed in Lau (1974a), if the "fixed" inputs are actually variable, the normalized restricted profit function can be interpreted as the first stage in a two-stage maximization problem, the second stage involving maximization with respect to the "fixed" inputs.[6]

The vintage of capital is included as a fixed input to allow for the effects of embodied technical change. Plants of different vintages may employ significantly different technologies. Inclusion of a vintage variable avoids possible biases resulting from differences in technology. Also, including the vintage variable makes it possible to test for the existence and neutrality of technical change.

The specification of the normalized restricted profit function is designed to reflect the major economic and technological characteristics of electric power generation. However, two potentially important influences on fuel choice could not be adequately treated in the specification. The first is the effect of environmental restrictions on fuel choice that exist in some areas. The second is the effect of changes in the temporal pattern of demand on fuel usage in plants that utilize different fuels for baseload and peak generation. These factors may have a significant effect on fuel choice, but data restrictions prevent their being incorporated in the model.

A convenient functional form for the normalized restricted profit function is the transcendental logarithmic (translog):

$$\ln \Pi = \alpha_\pi + \sum_i \alpha_i \ln P_i + \frac{1}{2} \sum_i \sum_h \gamma_{ih} \ln P_i \ln P_h + \sum_i \sum_j \delta_{ij} \ln P_i \ln Z_j$$

$$+ \sum_j \beta_j \ln Z_j + \frac{1}{2} \sum_j \sum_k \phi_{jk} \ln Z_j \ln Z_k \qquad i, h = C, O, G; j, k = K, L, T \qquad (6.1)$$

where $\gamma_{ih} = \gamma_{hi}$ and $\phi_{jk} = \phi_{kj}$. The translog is a flexible functional form in that it provides a second-order approximation to an arbitrary continuously twice-differentiable function.[7]

By Hotelling's lemma,

$$\frac{\partial \Pi}{\partial P_i} = -X_i^*$$

where X_i^* is the profit maximizing amount of input i (Diewert 1974). Using this lemma, logarithmic differentiation of the normalized restricted profit function yields demand equations for each fuel:

$$-\frac{\partial \ln \Pi}{\partial \ln P_i} = -\frac{\partial \Pi}{\partial P_i} \frac{P_i}{\Pi} = \frac{P_i X_i^*}{\Pi} = M_i =$$

$$-(\alpha_i + \sum_h \gamma_{ih} \ln P_h + \sum_j \delta_{ij} \ln Z_j) \qquad i, h = C, O, G; j = K, L, T \quad (6.2)$$

where M_i is the ratio of normalized expenditures on fuel i to normalized restricted profit.

The conditions $\gamma_{ih} = \gamma_{hi}$ and $\phi_{jk} = \phi_{kj}$ are often referred to as *symmetry conditions*. This terminology is potentially misleading, because these conditions are not necessary for symmetry of the translog form. Since the translog is a quadratic form, it can be made symmetric by the reparametrizations, $\gamma_{ih} = \frac{1}{2}(\gamma_{ih} + \gamma_{hi})$ and $\phi_{jk} = \frac{1}{2}(\phi_{jk} + \phi_{kj})$, and the parameters $\gamma_{ij} \neq \gamma_{ij}$ and $\phi_{jk} \neq \phi_{kj}$ cannot be identified econometrically.

Derivation of the demand equations from the normalized restricted profit function under the hypothesis of profit maximization does impose cross-equation equality restrictions on the γ_{ij}. To avoid misunderstanding, these restrictions will be referred to as *equality restrictions* rather than symmetry restrictions. However, it should be noted that these constraints do impose symmetry on the derivatives of the demand equations. Thus, $\partial X_i^*/\partial P_j = \partial X_j^*/\partial P_i$, as implied by economic theory. One of the major advantages of deriving systems of demand equations from flexible functional forms using duality theory is that the estimated elasticities of demand and substitution are subject only to those restrictions implied by economic theory.

The system of equations to be estimated consists of the normalized restricted profit equation, equation (6.1), and the fuel demand equations, equations (6.2). A classical additive disturbance term is included in each equation to reflect errors in profit-maximizing behavior. The imposition of cross-equation equality restrictions requires that the equations be estimated simultaneously. Since the off-diagonal elements of the residual convariance matrix can be expected to be nonzero, iterative Zellner-efficient estimation is used.[8] The estimates will be consistent under the assumption that all explanatory variables are exogenous.

A normalized restricted profit function is well behaved if it is strictly decreasing and convex in the normalized prices and strictly increasing in the fixed inputs. Lau (1974c) has proposed statistical tests for monotonicity and convexity, but computational problems in imposing the required nonnegativity constraints prevented their implementation. However, some indication of the extent to which the fitted restricted profit function is well behaved can be obtained by examining the regression results for each observation.

The condition that the restricted profit function be strictly decreasing in normalized prices is checked by examining the fitted expenditure ratios for positivity, since

$$M_i = -\frac{\partial \Pi}{\partial P_i} \frac{P_i}{\Pi}$$

and P_i and Π are positive for all observations in the sample. The condition that the restricted profit function be strictly increasing in fixed inputs is checked by calculating

$$\frac{\partial \Pi}{\partial Z_j} = \frac{\Pi}{Z_j} (\sum_i \delta_{ij} \ln P_i + \beta_j + \sum_k \phi_{jk} \ln Z_k)$$

$$i = C, O, G; j = K, L; k = K, L, T \quad (6.3)$$

for each observation.[9]

Convexity in prices requires that the Hessian of the restricted profit function be positive definite for each observation. This will be true if and only if all principal minors are positive. Convexity is checked for each observation by determining the signs of the estimated principal minors. Since it is not determined if any negative principal minors are statistically significant, this procedure does not constitute a statistical test of convexity.

The own- and cross-price elasticities of demand for fuels are readily derived from the estimated equations. The own-price elasticity is defined as

$$E_{ii} = \frac{\partial X_i^*}{\partial P_i} \frac{P_i}{X_i^*}$$

By Hotelling's lemma,

$$X_i^* = -\frac{\partial \Pi}{\partial P_i} \quad \text{and} \quad \frac{\partial X_i^*}{\partial P_i} = -\frac{\partial^2 \Pi}{\partial P_i^2}$$

Therefore,

$$E_{ii} = \frac{P_i \partial^2 \Pi / \partial P_i^2}{\partial \Pi / \partial P_i} = \frac{-M_i^2 - M_i - \gamma_{ii}}{M_i} \quad (6.4)$$

Similarly, the cross-price elasticity is equal to

$$E_{ih} = \frac{\partial X_i^*}{\partial P_h} \frac{P_h}{X_i^*} = \frac{P_h \partial^2 \Pi / \partial P_i \partial P_h}{\partial \Pi / \partial P_i} = \frac{-M_i M_h - \gamma_{ih}}{M_i} \quad (6.5)$$

Partial elasticities of substitution[10] are defined as

$$\sigma_{ii} = \frac{1}{M_i} E_{ii} = \frac{-M_i^2 - M_i - \gamma_{ii}}{M_i^2} \tag{6.6}$$

and

$$\sigma_{ih} = \frac{1}{M_h} E_{ih} = \frac{-M_i M_h - \gamma_{ih}}{M_i M_h} \tag{6.7}$$

The partial elasticities of substitution are normalized price elasticities, where the normalization is chosen such that the elasticities of substitution are invariant to the ordering of the factors. Therefore, $\sigma_{ih} = \sigma_{hi}$, although, in general, $E_{ih} \neq E_{hi}$.

Since the normalized restricted profit function is dual to the production function, estimation of the normalized restricted profit function can also provide information on other aspects of the technology. Of particular interest are tests of homotheticity and homogeneity of the production function and estimates of the degree of returns to scale.

The production function is homothetic if and only if the normalized restricted profit function satisfies the equation

$$-\Sigma P_i \frac{\partial \Pi}{\partial P_i} + \Sigma_j \frac{\partial \Pi}{\partial Z_j} = J(\Pi - \Sigma P_i \frac{\partial \Pi}{\partial P_i}) \quad i = C, O, G; j = K, L \tag{6.8}$$

where J is an arbitrary nonnegative and differentiable function defined on the nonnegative real line with $J(0) = 0$ (Lau 1974d). Necessary and sufficient conditions for the translog function to satisfy equation (6.8) are

$$\lambda \Sigma_i \gamma_{ir} + \Sigma_j \delta_{jr} = \sigma \alpha_r \tag{6.9}$$

and

$$\lambda \Sigma_i \delta_{is} + \Sigma_j \phi_{js} = \sigma \beta_s \quad i, r = C, O, G; j, s = K, L \tag{6.10}$$

where $\sigma \equiv J'(1 - \Sigma_i \frac{\partial \ln \Pi}{\partial \ln P_i}) - \frac{J}{\Pi} \quad i = C, O, G$

$\lambda \equiv J' - 1$

at the point of approximation.[11]

The production function is homogeneous of degree k, a scalar constant, if and only if the normalized restricted profit function satisfies the equation

$$-\Sigma_i P_i \frac{\partial \Pi}{\partial P_i} + \Sigma_j \frac{\partial \Pi}{\partial Z_j} Z_j = k(\Pi - \Sigma_i P_i \frac{\partial \Pi}{\partial P_i}) \quad i = C, O, G; j = K, L$$

(6.11)

which is a specialization of equation (6.8). When the normalized restricted profit function satisfies equation (6.11), J' is a constant everywhere, not just at the point of expansion, and the value of J' is equal to the degree of returns to scale, k. Since

$$J = J'\Pi(1 - \Sigma_i \frac{\partial \ln \Pi}{\partial \ln P_i}) \quad i = C, O, G$$

σ in equations (6.9) and (6.10) is equal to zero. Therefore, homogeneity can be tested by adding one additional restriction to those for homotheticity, and the degree of returns to scale can be determined by calculating $k = J' = \lambda + 1$.

The production function is also tested for groupwise homotheticity and homogeneity. The production function is homothetic in the variable inputs if and only if the normalized restricted profit function satisfies

$$\Sigma_i \gamma_{ih} = \sigma \alpha_h \quad i, h = C, O, G$$

The production function is homogeneous of degree k in the variable inputs if and only if the normalized restricted profit function is homogeneous of degree $-k/(1 - k)$ in normalized prices (Lau 1969). This will be true if and only if

$$\Sigma_i \gamma_{ih} = 0 \quad \Sigma_i^3 \delta_{ij} = 0 \quad i, h = C, O, G; j = K, L$$

(6.12)

The normalized restricted profit function also can be used to test hypotheses concerning the characteristics of technical change in electric power generation. If the production function is homothetic, Hicksian neutrality of the normalized restricted profit function implies Hicksian neutrality of the production function (Lau 1969). If the production function is not homothetic, Hicksian neutrality of the normalized restricted profit function implies that technical change is "output augmenting" and "factor saving" at equal rates. The normalized restricted profit function will be Hicksian neutral if

$$\delta_{iT} = 0 \quad \phi_{jT} = 0 \quad i = C, O, G; j = K, L$$

(6.13)

The absence of technical change implies restrictions (6.13) plus

$$\phi_{TT} = 0 \qquad \beta_T = 0 \qquad\qquad (6.14)$$

In performing the tests of hypotheses, the system of equations is estimated with and without the relevant restrictions imposed. The results are compared by computing $-2 \log L$, where L is the ratio of the maximum value of the likelihood function for the restricted equations to the maximum value of the likelihood function for the unrestricted equations. Under the null hypothesis being tested, this statistic is distributed asymptotically as chi-squared with degrees of freedom equal to the number of restrictions.[12]

Energy Substitution in Manufacturing

Manufacturing industries account for approximately one-fourth the total energy consumed as fuel in the United States.[13] Considerable shifts have occurred in the composition of the manufacturing sector's energy consumption in recent years. For example, between 1958 and 1971 the shares of electricity and gas in total purchases of energy increased approximately 30 percent, while the share of coal decreased 58 percent. The model developed here makes it possible to estimate the extent to which shifts in the composition of energy consumption in manufacturing are due to changes in relative energy prices.

Since the characteristics of energy demand can be expected to vary across industries, energy substitution in manufacturing is studied at the level of individual two-digit industries. A continuously twice-differentiable aggregate production function is assumed to exist at the state level for each two-digit industry,

$$Y = Y(E, O, G, C, X)$$

where Y is total output, E is electricity, O is fuel oil, G is gas, C is coal, and X is a vector of all other inputs.

Nonenergy inputs cannot be included explicitly in the empirical model because adequate cross-section data are not available for recent years. The omission of nonenergy inputs will not bias the estimated energy elasticities if the production function is homothetically weakly separable in the energy inputs.[14] In this case the production function can be written

$$Y = Y[H(E, O, G, C), X]$$

where H is an energy-input aggregator function.

Given homothetic weak separability as a maintained hypothesis, the characteristics of energy substitution might be analyzed by estimating the parameters of the energy-input aggregator function. One difficulty that would arise using this approach is that aggregate energy input cannot be directly observed. An index of aggregate energy input could be computed, but serious statistical difficulties would remain because of the endogeneity of the explanatory variables. Therefore, duality theory is used to derive the energy demand equations from an energy cost function.[15]

The energy cost function dual to the energy-input function can be written

$$W = W(H, P_E, P_O, P_G, P_C)$$

where W is total cost of energy, H is aggregate energy input, and P_E, P_O, P_G, and P_C are the prices of electricity, fuel oil, gas, and coal, respectively. If the energy-input function is a positive, nondecreasing, positively linear homogeneous, concave function, the energy cost function can be written

$$W = H \cdot V(P_E, P_O, P_G, P_C)$$

where V is a unit cost function satisfying the same regularity conditions (Diewert 1973).

As discussed in Lau (1974a), duality exists between the cost and production functions under less restrictive assumptions on the production function. The assumptions used here ensure that the cost function has desirable properties for the particular problem being studied. In particular, the assumption that the aggregator function is linear homogeneous permits the use of a unit cost function, which eliminates the need for data on aggregate energy input.

A convenient functional form for the unit cost function is the translog

$$\ln V = \alpha_v + \sum_i \alpha_i \ln P_i + \frac{1}{2} \sum_i \sum_j \gamma_{ij} \ln P_i \ln P_j \quad i, j = E, O, G, C$$

$$(6.15)$$

where $\gamma_{ij} = \gamma_{ji}$. The translog unit cost function does not satisfy the regularity conditions globally unless all $\gamma_{ij} = 0$, i.e., unless it collapses into a Cobb-Douglas form. However, the estimated cost function can be checked to determine if the regularity conditions are satisfied in the relevant region.

By Shepard's lemma,

$$X_i^* = H \frac{\partial V}{\partial P_i} \quad i = E, O, G, C \qquad (6.16)$$

where X_i^* is the cost minimizing quantity of energy input i (Diewert 1974). Using Shepard's lemma, demand equations are obtained by logarithmic differentiation of the unit cost function:

$$\frac{\partial \ln V}{\partial \ln P_i} = \frac{\partial V}{\partial P_i} \frac{P_i}{V} = \alpha_i + \sum_j \gamma_{ij} \ln P_j \quad i, j = E, O, G, C \quad (6.17)$$

Since the cost function is linear homogeneous in prices, $W = \sum_i P_i X_i^*$ by Euler's theorem. Therefore, $V = \sum_i P_i X_i^*/H$. Also, from equation (6.16), $\partial V/\partial P_i = X_i^*/H$. Substituting in equation (6.17),

$$\frac{\partial \ln V}{\partial \ln P_i} = \frac{P_i X_i^*/H}{\sum_i P_i X_i^*/H} = \frac{P_i X_i^*}{\sum_i P_i X_i^*} = M_i \quad i = E, O, G, C \quad (6.18)$$

where M_i is the cost share for input i. Thus, derivation of the energy demand equation from a unit cost function eliminates the need for data on aggregate energy input, H.

The complete system of cost share equations is

$$M_E = \alpha_E + \gamma_{EE} \ln P_E + \gamma_{EO}^E \ln P_O + \gamma_{EG}^E \ln P_G + \gamma_{EC}^E \ln P_C + u_E$$
$$M_O = \alpha_O + \gamma_{EO}^O \ln P_E + \gamma_{OO} \ln P_O + \gamma_{OG}^O \ln P_G + \gamma_{OC}^O \ln P_C + u_O$$
$$M_G = \alpha_G + \gamma_{EG}^G \ln P_E + \gamma_{OG}^G \ln P_O + \gamma_{GG} \ln P_G + \gamma_{GC}^G \ln P_C + u_G$$
$$M_C = \alpha_C + \gamma_{EC}^C \ln P_E + \gamma_{OC}^C \ln P_O + \gamma_{GC}^C \ln P_G + \gamma_{CC} \ln P_C + u_C$$

where the additive disturbance terms, u_i, are included to reflect random errors in cost minimizing behavior. Because the cost shares sum to unity at each observation, the parameters must satisfy the following adding-up restrictions:

$$\alpha_E + \alpha_O + \alpha_G + \alpha_C = 1$$
$$\gamma_{EE} + \gamma_{EO}^O + \gamma_{EG}^G + \gamma_{EC}^C = 0$$
$$\gamma_{EO}^E + \gamma_{OO} + \gamma_{OG}^G + \gamma_{OC}^C = 0 \quad (6.20)$$
$$\gamma_{EG}^E + \gamma_{OG}^O + \gamma_{GG} + \gamma_{GC}^C = 0$$
$$\gamma_{EC}^E + \gamma_{OC}^O + \gamma_{GC}^G + \gamma_{CC} = 0$$

Therefore, only 15 of the 20 parameters are free, and parameter estimates for all four share equations can be derived from the parameter estimates for any three.

Derivation of the share equations from the unit cost function, equation (6.15), implies the following cross-equation equality restrictions[16] on the γ_{ij}:

$$\gamma_{EO}^E = \gamma_{EO}^O$$
$$\gamma_{EG}^E = \gamma_{EG}^G$$
$$\gamma_{EC}^E = \gamma_{EC}^C$$
$$\gamma_{OG}^O = \gamma_{OG}^G \qquad (6.21)$$
$$\gamma_{OC}^O = \gamma_{OC}^C$$
$$\gamma_{GC}^G = \gamma_{GC}^C$$

The cross-equation equality restrictions reduce the number of free parameters to nine. Imposition of these restrictions requires that the equations be estimated simultaneously. Since the cost shares necessarily sum to unity, the sum of the disturbances across the four equations is zero at each observation, and the disturbance covariance matrix is singular. Therefore, one equation must be omitted from the system.

The choice of the equation to be omitted is arbitrary. The disturbance term from the equation for M_C is dropped and this equation is omitted from the system. Because γ_{EC}^C, γ_{OC}^C, and γ_{GC}^C do not appear in the remaining three equations, an alternative set of cross-equation equality constraints is required for these parameters. Substituting in (6.21) from (6.20),

$$\gamma_{EC}^E = -(\gamma_{EE} + \gamma_{EO}^O + \gamma_{EG}^G)$$
$$\gamma_{OC}^O = -(\gamma_{EO}^E + \gamma_{OO} + \gamma_{OG}^G) \qquad (6.22)$$
$$\gamma_{GC}^G = -(\gamma_{EG}^E + \gamma_{OG}^O + \gamma_{GG})$$

Solving (6.22) for γ_{EE}, γ_{OO}, and γ_{GG} and substituting in (6.19), the system of equations to be estimated is

$$
\begin{aligned}
M_E &= \alpha_E + \gamma_{EO}(\ln P_O - \ln P_E) + \gamma_{EG}(\ln P_G - \ln P_E) \\
&\quad + \gamma_{EC}(\ln P_C - \ln P_E) + u_E \\
M_O &= \alpha_O + \gamma_{EO}(\ln P_E - \ln P_O) + \gamma_{OG}(\ln P_G - \ln P_O) \\
&\quad + \gamma_{OC}(\ln P_C - \ln P_O) + u_O \\
M_G &= \alpha_G + \gamma_{EG}(\ln P_E - \ln P_G) + \gamma_{OG}(\ln P_O - \ln P_G) \\
&\quad + \gamma_{GC}(\ln P_C - \ln P_G) + u_G
\end{aligned}
\qquad (6.23)
$$

Estimates of the omitted parameters, γ_{EE}, γ_{OO}, γ_{GG}, and γ_{CC} can be calculated from (6.20).[17]

The vector of disturbance terms, (u_C, u_O, u_G), is assumed to be independently and identically normally distributed with mean vector zero and nonsingular covariance matrix Ω. The system of three share equations is estimated with an iterative Zellner-efficient procedure, which is equivalent to maximum-likelihood estimation. Therefore, the parameter estimates are invariant to the choice of equation to be omitted from the system.

The equations are estimated with cross-section state data for 1971, 1962, and 1958. The system of cost share equations derived from the four-input unit cost function cannot be estimated for all two-digit industries because data on coal consumption are not available for a sufficient number of states for some industries. Restricting the model to electricity, fuel oil, and gas is appropriate if the production function is weakly separable in these three inputs. The separability of these inputs from coal is tested statistically for those industries for which the four-input model is estimated.

Weak separability of the (homogeneous) energy-input function in E, O, and G implies weak separability of the unit cost function in P_E, P_O, and P_G. However, the translog approximation of a weakly separable cost function is not necessarily weakly separable. The conditions on the translog unit cost function corresponding to weak separability of the true unit cost function in P_E, P_O, and P_G from P_C are

$$\gamma_{EC} = \theta\alpha_E$$
$$\gamma_{OC} = \theta\alpha_O \qquad (6.24)$$
$$\gamma_{GC} = \theta\alpha_G$$

Explicit separability of the translog function itself requires the further restriction, $\theta = 0$, in (6.24).[18]

As previously noted, the unrestricted translog unit cost function does not satisfy the regularity conditions globally. Imposition of the equality restrictions on the γ_{ij} together with the adding-up restrictions ensures that the unit cost function is linear homogeneous in the input prices. However, the fitted unit cost function may or may not satisfy the conditions that it be nondecreasing and concave.

The fitted unit cost function is nondecreasing in the input prices if the fitted shares are nonnegative, since

$$M_i = \frac{\partial V}{\partial P_i} \frac{P_i}{V} \qquad i = E, O, G, C$$

and P_i and V are always positive. Concavity of the unit cost function requires that the Hessian matrix be negative semidefinite for each observation. This will be true if the first $n - 1$ ordered principal minors alternate in sign. The nth order principal minor will be zero because of the imposition of linear homogeneity in input prices.[19] Concavity is checked for each observation by calculating the values of the principal minors. Since it is not determined if the principal minors are statistically significant, this procedure does not constitute a statistical test of concavity.

Estimates of the own- and cross-price eleasticities of demand are calculated from the estimated cost share equations. The own-price elasticity of demand for energy input i is defined as

$$E_{ii} = \frac{\partial X_i^*}{\partial P_i} \frac{P_i}{X_i^*}$$

Applying Shepard's lemma to obtain expressions for X_i^* and $\partial X_i^*/\partial P_i$ in terms of derivatives of the unit cost function, the own-price elasticity can be rewritten,

$$E_{ii} = \frac{P_i \partial^2 V/\partial P_i^2}{\partial V/\partial P_i} = \frac{M_i^2 - M_i + \gamma_{ii}}{M_i} \qquad i = E, O, G, C \qquad (6.25)$$

Similarly, the cross-price elasticity of demand for input i with respect to the price of input j is

$$E_{ij} = \frac{\partial X_i^*}{\partial P_j} \frac{P_j}{X_i^*} = \frac{P_j \partial^2 V/\partial P_i \partial P_j}{\partial V/\partial P_i} = \frac{M_i M_j + \gamma_{ij}}{M_i} \qquad i, j = E, O, G, C \qquad (6.26)$$

Allen cross-partial elasticities of substitution are equal to

$$\sigma_{ij} = \frac{1}{M_j} E_{ij} = \frac{M_i M_j + \gamma_{ij}}{M_i M_j} \qquad i, j = E, O, G, C \qquad (6.27)$$

Thus the Allen cross-elasticities can be interpreted as normalized cross-price elasticities, where the normalization is chosen such that the elasticity of substitution is invariant to the ordering of the factors.

Price elasticities estimated using a unit cost function for energy measure the extent of price responsiveness holding aggregate energy input constant. This is clearly not equal to the total price responsiveness, since a change in the price of a type of energy will affect the price of aggregate energy and thus will affect total energy input. Treating aggregate energy input as variable, the effect of a change in the price of energy input j on the quantity of energy input i is

$$E_{ij}^T = E_{ij} + E_{iH} E_{Hj}$$

where E_{ij} is the price elasticity holding aggregate energy, H, constant, E_{iH} is the elasticity of demand for energy input i with respect to aggregate energy, and E_{Hj} is the elasticity of demand for aggregate energy with respect to the price of energy input j.

Since the energy-input function is assumed to be linear homogeneous, E_{iH} is equal to unity. Also,

$$E_{Hj} = \frac{\partial \ln H}{\partial \ln V} \frac{\partial \ln V}{\partial \ln P_j} = E_{HV} M_j$$

where E_{HV} is the elasticity of demand for aggregate energy with respect to the price of aggregate energy. Therefore,

$$E_{ij}^T = E_{ij} + E_{HV} M_j \tag{6.28}$$

Thus, given estimates of the own-price elasticity of demand for aggregate energy, E_{HV}, the total responsiveness of each type of energy to price changes can be calculated from the elasticities estimated using a unit cost function.[20]

Concluding Comments

The derivation of energy demand models for electric power generation and for manufacturing illustrates the usefulness of duality theory in applied economic research. Because duality theory provides alternative representations of the technology, the models can be designed to reflect the particular characteristics of the problem at hand. Also, by allowing the use of flexible functional forms, duality theory makes it possible to obtain estimates of elasticities of demand and substitution subject only to those restrictions implied by economic theory.

Estimation procedures and results for the model of interfuel substitution in electric power generation are discussed in Chapter 7. The results for energy substitution in manufacturing industries are discussed in Chapter 8.

Notes

1. See Atkinson and Halvorsen (1976b, 1977); Berndt and Jorgenson (1973); Berndt and Wood (1975); Binswanger (1974); Burgess (1974); Christensen and Greene (1976); Christensen and Manser (1977); Christensen, Jorgenson, and Lau (1971, 1973); Diamond and McFadden (1974); Diewert (1971, 1973, 1974, 1976); Fuss (1977); Halvorsen and Ford (1978); Jorgenson and Lau (1975); Lau (1969, 1974b); Lau and Yotopoulos (1971); Parks (1971); and Yotopoulos and Lau (1973).

2. A functional form is defined to be *flexible* if it is capable of providing a second order approximation to an arbitrary continuously twice-differentiable function, see Diewert (1974), and Lau (1974*b*).

3. This section is based on Atkinson and Halvorsen (1976*a*).

4. See Averch and Johnson (1962). Bailey (1973) and Baumol and Klevorick (1970) provide surveys of the theoretical literature on the effects of rate-of-return regulation. Empirical studies include Atkinson and Halvorsen (1977), Courville (1974), and Spann (1974).

5. Barzel (1964) and Dhrymes and Kurz (1964) present evidence that labor is largely fixed in existing plants. Fuss (1971) concludes that the hypothesis of a putty-clay technology cannot be rejected for a model incorporating capital, labor, and a fuel aggregate.

6. However, if the quantities of capital and labor are actually variable, treating them as exogenous in the estimation procedure is not appropriate.

7. The translog form was introduced by Christensen, Jorgenson, and Lau (1971, 1973).

8. See Zellner (1962). Iterative Zellner-efficient estimation is equivalent to maximum-likelihood estimation, see Oberhofer and Kmenta (1974).

9. By Hotelling's lemma, equation (6.3) provides estimates of the shadow prices of the fixed inputs.

10. The partial elasticities defined here are analogous but not identical to Allen (1966) partial elasticities of substitution. They differ in that quantities rather than prices of fixed factors are held constant.

11. The point of approximation is the geometric mean of the sample.

12. Berndt and Savin (1977) examine alternative test statistics in the multivariate linear regression model and find that the value of the likelihood-ratio test statistic lies between the values of the Wald and Lagrange multiplier test statistics.

13. Parts of this section are taken from Halvorsen (1977). Research for this section was supported by an NSF-RANN grant to the National Bureau of Economic Research.

14. Separability of energy inputs from capital and labor inputs is tested statistically with 1958 data in Halvorsen and Ford (1978). Weak separability is accepted for all industries for which the model incorporating capital and labor inputs performs well. These industries account for approximately one-half total energy consumption in manufacturing.

15. A cost function is used rather than a normalized restricted profit function because of the unavailability of adequate data on the quantities of the nonenergy inputs and the price of output.

16. The adding-up restrictions together with the cross-equation equality restrictions on the γ_{ij} impose linear homogeneity in prices on the unit cost function.

17. The parameter estimates obtained from estimation of the cost share equations can be used in (6.15) to compute the unit cost of aggregate energy up

to a scalar constant. Alternatively, the unit cost of aggregate energy can be indexed using superlative index numbers; see Diewert (1976).

18. Jorgenson and Lau (1975) develop these restrictions in the context of translog utility functions. The test for implicit separability is exact only at the point of approximation. However, the test for explicit separability is invariant to the scaling of the price variables.

19. The condition that the first $n - 1$ ordered principal minors alternate in sign is sufficient for negative semidefiniteness only if the first $n - 1$ ordered principal minors are all different from zero.

20. The use of a normalized restricted profit function in estimating elasticities of demand for fuels in electric power generation provides direct measures of the total responsiveness of demand (with capital and labor fixed) because output is not held constant in a profit function.

7 Interfuel Substitution in Electric Power Generation

Introduction

Approximately one-fifth the United States' total energy consumption is in the form of electric energy produced from fossil fuels. The derived demand for fuels to be used in generating electric energy accounts for approximately two-thirds the coal, one-tenth the oil, and one-fifth the natural gas consumed as fuel. Thus an understanding of the determinants of the demand for fuels by electric utilities is necessary for informed decision making with respect to public policies toward energy. Other characteristics of the production process for electric energy are also relevant for the formulation and evaluation of public policies. In particular, the extent of increasing returns to scale is important in determining appropriate regulatory policies.

There have been many econometric studies of steam electric power generation, but the existing studies do not provide adequate information on demand for fuels in electric power generation.[1] The most important shortcoming of previous studies is that all types of fuel have generally been aggregated into a single fuel input, precluding the possibility of estimating elasticities of substitution between fuels. The only studies to examine interfuel substitution are Lawrence (1972) and Joskow and Mishkin (1974). Lawrence uses a branched CES production function to analyze interfuel substitution separately from capital and labor. His main emphasis is on estimation procedures, and little information is provided on the estimated elasticities of substitution. Joskow and Mishkin assume that there are a limited number of fixed-coefficient technologies available to utilities and use a logit model to estimate the extent of substitution ex ante. Interfuel substitution in existing plants is not examined.

Another major shortcoming of previous studies is that production possibilities are generally specified by restrictive functional forms, imposing severe a priori constraints on elasticities of substitution as well as other characteristics of the production process.[2] Also, previous studies have generally assumed a putty-clay technology and have not explored the possibilities of input substitution in existing plants.[3]

The present study directly addresses these issues. Coal, oil, and gas are treated as different inputs. To avoid imposing a priori restrictions on the characteristics of production, a translog normalized restricted profit function is estimated. Duality theory allows characteristics of the production function to be deduced from the estimated profit function. Finally, a putty-clay technology is not assumed for fuel inputs.

Since the assumption that little or no interfuel substitution can occur in existing plants is very common, it is useful to consider the mechanisms by which such substitution can occur. First, individual generating units may be designed to be able to utilize more than one type of fuel. Second, a plant generally contains more than one generating unit, and different units may utilize different fuels. Units are brought on-line in rank order according to their marginal cost of generation. Changes in fuel prices alter the relative marginal cost of units using different fuels, and thereby affect the proportion of output produced with each type of fuel.

The estimated elasticities of demand and substitution reported in this chapter indicate that substantial interfuel substitution occurs in existing plants. The model used also permits tests of other characteristics of the production process. The results indicate that the production function is predominantly homogeneous, the degree of increasing returns to scale is not great, and shifts in the production function resulting from embodied technical change have been slight.

Estimation Procedures

The derivation of the model used here is discussed in Chapter 6. The system of equations to be estimated consists of a translog normalized restricted profit function,

$$\ln \Pi = \alpha_\pi + \sum_i \alpha_i \ln P_i + \frac{1}{2} \sum_i \sum_h \gamma_{ih} \ln P_i \ln P_h + \sum_i \sum_j \delta_{ij} \ln P_i \ln Z_j$$
$$+ \sum_j \beta_j \ln Z_j + \frac{1}{2} \sum_j \sum_k \phi_{jk} \ln Z_j \ln Z_k \quad i, h = C, O, G; j, k = K, L, T \quad (7.1)$$

where $\gamma_{ih} = \gamma_{hi}$ and $\phi_{jk} = \phi_{kj}$, and the associated demand equations

$$M_i = -(\alpha_i + \sum_h \gamma_{ih} \ln P_h + \sum_j \delta_{ij} \ln Z_j) \quad i, h = C, O, G; j = K, L, T \quad (7.2)$$

where M_i is the ratio of normalized expenditures on input i to normalized restricted profit. The P_i are the normalized prices of the variable inputs, coal, C, oil, O, and gas, G, and the Z_j are the quantities of the fixed inputs, capital, K, labor, L, and vintage of capital, T.

The normalized restricted profit function could be estimated by itself using ordinary least squares, but doing so would neglect the additional information contained in the demand equations. The procedure used here is to jointly estimate the normalized restricted profit function and the demand equations as a multivariate regression system.[4] Including the demand equations in the estimation procedure has the effect of adding additional degrees of freedom without adding any new parameters to be estimated.[5] The result is an increase in the efficiency of the parameter estimates compared to those obtained by estimating only the profit function.

The system of equations is estimated using an iterative Zellner-efficient procedure. The data used are for individual conventional steam electric plants and, unless noted otherwise, are for 1972. The data are from U.S. Federal Power Commission (FPC) publications (1973a, 1973b, 1974).

Normalized fuel prices are calculated by dividing cost per million Btu by the price of output. Data on expenditure per million Btu for each type of fuel are from FPC (1974). In order to partially reflect the effect of environmental restrictions on fuel costs, the price of coal is adjusted by adding the cost per million Btu of ash removal. Data on the cost of ash removal are for 1970 and are from FPC (1973b).

Data on the price of output are not available at the plant level. Therefore, data from FPC (1973a) for the firm owning each plant are used. To obtain a measure of the net value of plant output to the firm, output price is calculated by dividing total revenue minus transmission and distribution expenses by total sales.

The average number of employees for each plant from FPC (1974) is used as the measure of labor input. The quantity of capital is equal to installed generating capacity, which is measured by the manufacturer's maximum nameplate rating (FPC 1974). The vintage of the capital for each plant is calculated by weighting the vintage of each generating unit by its capacity (FPC 1974). Normalized restricted profit is calculated as net generation (FPC 1974) minus normalized expenditures on fuels.

The sample includes all plants beginning operation in 1946 or later for which the necessary data are available. Data on fuel prices are available only for plants actually purchasing the fuels in question. Therefore, the sample had to be restricted to plants purchasing more than one type of fuel. The number of plants using all three fuels is too small for estimation of the system of profit and demand equations. Therefore, separate sets of equations are estimated for each pair of fuels: coal-gas, coal-oil, and oil-gas.

The exclusion of plants using only one type of fuel in 1972 may bias the estimated elasticities of demand and substitution. The direction of the bias, if any, is not clear. Plants using only one fuel may have gone to the extreme of substituting entirely away from other fuels, or may not be able to use more than one fuel. Estimated elasticities would be biased downward in the former case and upward in the latter case.

Performance of the Model

Parameter estimates and asymptotic standard errors for the system of normalized restricted profit and input demand equations estimated for each pair of fuels are shown in Table 7-1. The number of observations is 31 for the coal-gas sample, 17 for the coal-oil sample, and 60 for the oil-gas sample. The table also shows the value of $\bar{R}^2$ for each equation, where R^2 is computed as one minus the ratio of the residual sum of squares to the total sum of squares and then adjusted for the number of parameters estimated. The calculated $\bar{R}^2$'s are quite high for cross-section equations fitted with microdata. However, the estimated standard errors are also quite large, and only 21 of the 60 estimated parameters are significant at the 5 percent level.

The condition that the restricted profit function be decreasing in the prices of variable inputs implies that the fitted expenditure ratios should be positive All but 2 of the 62 fitted ratios are positive for the coal-gas sample, and all are positive for the oil-gas sample. The coal-oil sample performs somewhat less well, with 6 of the 34 fitted ratios negative.

A second condition for a well-behaved restricted profit function is that the partial derivatives of restricted profit with respect to fixed inputs be positive. The calculated values of the derivative with respect to capital are all positive for the three samples. The results for the derivative of restricted profit with respect to labor are less satisfactory. Of the calculated derivatives, 16 are negative for the coal-gas and oil-gas samples, and 8 are negative for the coal-oil sample. This may be due to the poor quality of the data on labor input, which is measured as average number of employees per year with no adjustment for the number of hours worked per employee.

Convexity of the normalized restricted profit function is checked by determining if the values of the principal minors of the estimated Hessian are positive. Negative values were found for 9 observations in the coal-gas sample, 10 in the coal-oil sample, and 52 in the oil-gas sample. Thus it appears that the restricted profit function fails to satisfy the convexity condition for a substantial number of observations. Since convexity is implied by the assumption of profit maximization, this is a serious weakness in the performance of the model. Tests of the equality restrictions relating parameters in the profit and demand equations also cast doubt on the performance of the model. These restrictions, which are also implied by profit maximization, were rejected for the coal-gas and coal-oil samples.[6]

There are several possible reasons for the problems with convexity and equality. As discussed in Chapter 6, the model does not explicitly incorporate the full effects on fuel choice of environmental restrictions or of changes in plant load factors. Also, there are serious weaknesses in the data used. In particular, output price for each plant had to be approximated by dividing the firm's total revenue minus transmission and distribution expenses by total sales. This

Table 7-1
Estimates of Parameters of the Normalized Restricted Profit Function

Parameter	Coal-Gas Sample		Coal-Oil Sample		Oil-Gas Sample	
	Estimate	Stan. Error	Estimate	Stan. Error	Estimate	Stan. Error
α_π	62.765[a]	27.655	−59.843	41.160	−11.218	23.869
α_C	0.658[a]	0.398	1.291[a]	0.758	N/E	N/E
α_O	N/E	N/E	−6.049[a]	1.668	1.405[a]	0.653
α_G	−0.422	0.289	N/E	N/E	0.351	0.452
γ_{CC}	−0.263[a]	0.048	−0.024	0.082	N/E	N/E
γ_{OO}	N/E	N/E	0.064	0.163	0.073	0.061
γ_{GG}	0.023	0.030	N/E	N/E	−0.324[a]	0.052
γ_{CG}	−0.046	0.028	N/E	N/E	N/E	N/E
γ_{CO}	N/E	N/E	−0.309[a]	0.058	N/E	N/E
γ_{OG}	N/E	N/E	N/E	N/E	−0.167[a]	0.041
δ_{CK}	−0.016	0.033	−0.020	0.045	N/E	N/E
δ_{CL}	−0.008	0.038	−0.025	0.060	N/E	N/E
δ_{CT}	0.074	0.047	0.044	0.056	N/E	N/E
δ_{OK}	N/E	N/E	−0.461[a]	0.154	0.085[a]	0.042
δ_{OL}	N/E	N/E	0.551[a]	0.135	−0.144[a]	0.062
δ_{OT}	N/E	N/E	1.028[a]	0.212	−0.055	0.065
δ_{GK}	0.003	0.024	N/E	N/E	−0.011	0.029
δ_{GL}	0.021	0.027	N/E	N/E	0.083[a]	0.041
δ_{GT}	0.058	0.034	N/E	N/E	0.044	0.043
β_K	3.405	3.671	−4.378	2.293	−4.452	3.116
β_L	−5.428	4.842	15.791[a]	7.076	5.387	4.756
β_T	−15.736[a]	6.508	3.410	3.116	5.427	4.970
ϕ_{KK}	−0.061	0.318	0.295	0.186	−0.573	0.298
ϕ_{LL}	0.107	0.426	−1.591[a]	0.636	−0.571	0.486
ϕ_{TT}	1.034	0.743	−0.563[a]	0.281	−0.358	0.642
ϕ_{KT}	−0.866	0.483	−0.150	0.257	0.606	0.364
ϕ_{KL}	0.025	0.347	0.469[a]	0.235	0.586	0.331
ϕ_{LT}	1.449[a]	0.613	−0.411	0.283	−0.655	0.503
Equation $\bar{R}^2$						
Profit	0.95		0.96		0.89	
Coal	0.75		0.69		—	
Oil	—		0.44		0.17	
Gas	0.37		—		0.40	

[a]Significant at the .05 level.
N/E means not estimated for this sample.

measure of the value of output can be expected to result in an overstatement of normalized restricted profit for some plants and an understatement for others. Lastly, the cross-section data used may include observations that are too far from the point of approximation of the translog function to the true profit function. These shortcomings should be kept in mind in evaluating the results presented below.

Elasticity Estimates

Estimates of all own- and cross-price elasticities of demand for each plant are shown in Tables 7-2 through 7-4. Plants are listed in order of increasing size. There is no obvious relationship between the magnitudes of the estimated elasticities and plant size.

The number of own-price elasticities with the correct (negative) sign is 50 of 62 for the coal-gas sample, 33 of 34 for the coal-oil sample, and 120 of 160 for the oil-gas sample. The incorrect signs for the remaining estimated own-price elasticities reflect the apparent failure of the profit function to be convex for all observations.

Table 7-2
Estimates of Price Elasticities: Coal-Gas Sample[a]

Plant[b]	E_{CC}	E_{CG}	E_{GC}	E_{GG}
1	−0.67	−0.05	−0.10	−1.31
2	0.85	0.27	0.47	−1.38
3	0.16	0.15	0.32	−1.35
4	−0.21	0.09	0.27	−1.35
5	−0.94	−0.05	−0.17	−1.31
6	−0.80	0.02	0.12	−1.36
7	−0.26	0.08	0.25	−1.35
8	−1.02	−0.04	−0.18	−1.31
9	0.69	0.28	0.95	−1.60
10	0.05	0.16	0.49	−1.42
11	−0.84	0.001	0.01	−1.33
12	−0.28	0.08	0.22	−1.34
13	−0.77	0.03	0.15	−1.37
14	−0.80	0.02	0.12	−1.36
15	−0.02	0.17	1.07	−1.69
16	−0.95	−0.001	−0.005	−1.34
17	−0.71	0.07	0.49	−1.50
18	0.33	0.22	0.86	−1.57
19	−0.58	0.09	0.77	−1.60
20	−0.64	0.10	1.07	−1.76
21	−0.35	0.15	2.30	−2.32
22	6.04	1.21	41.17	−21.86
23	−0.62	0.09	0.83	−1.64
24	−0.60	0.09	0.67	−1.56
25	−0.88	0.01	0.04	−1.35
26	0.19	0.22	1.64	−1.95
27	−0.32	0.14	1.20	−1.78
28	−0.55	0.11	1.13	−1.77
29	−0.48	0.12	1.62	−2.00
30	0.03	0.22	−7.05	2.47
31	7.43	1.51	−1.46	−0.25

[a]E_{ij} indicates the elasticity of demand for fuel i with respect to the price of fuel j.
[b]Listed in increasing order of size.

Table 7-3
Estimates of Price Elasticities: Coal-Oil Sample[a]

Plant[b]	E_{CC}	E_{CO}	E_{OC}	E_{OO}
1	−1.02	1.65	1.10	−1.50
2	−1.20	0.52	0.27	−1.67
3	−1.41	−0.87	−0.26	−2.58
4	−0.94	2.26	1.41	−1.52
5	−1.20	1.30	−1.72	−0.49
6	−0.97	2.09	2.14	−1.60
7	−1.04	0.96	0.22	−1.87
8	−1.19	0.81	0.74	−1.51
9	−1.25	1.01	−6.48	0.32
10	−1.06	1.05	0.34	−1.70
11	−1.18	0.91	1.08	−1.51
12	−1.21	1.49	−1.02	−0.43
13	−0.28	9.89	−1.95	−0.44
14	−1.36	0.87	−2.94	−0.36
15	−1.35	0.88	−2.86	−0.37
16	−0.23	10.14	0.98	−1.51
17	−1.39	0.50	1.12	−1.52

[a]E_{ij} indicates the elasticity of demand for fuel i with respect to the price of fuel j.
[b]Listed in increasing order of size.

The cross-price elasticities of demand will be positive for pairs of fuels that are substitutes, and negative for pairs that are complements. The estimated cross-price elasticities indicate that the predominant relationship among fuels is that of substitutes, as would be expected.[7] All the estimated cross-price elasticities are positive for the oil-gas sample, 52 of 62 estimates are positive for the coal-gas sample, and 26 of 34 are positive for the coal-oil sample.

Estimates of the cross-elasticities of substitution for each plant are shown in Table 7-5. There is considerably more variation in magnitude for the estimated elasticities of substitution than for the estimated elasticities of demand. The estimated elasticities of substitution are computed by dividing the estimated elasticities of demand by the ratio of normalized expenditure on a fuel to normalized restricted profit, see equation (6.27). The greater variation in the elasticities of substitution reflects the variation in this ratio across both fuels and observations

Estimates of elasticities of demand and substitution evaluated at the means of the data are shown in Table 7-6, together with their estimated standard errors.[8] Five of the six estimated own-price elasticities have the correct sign, of which all are significant at the 5 percent level. The estimate with an incorrect sign is not significant. All the six estimated cross-price elasticities are positive, and five are significant at the 5 percent level. The three estimated cross-elasticities of substitution are all positive, and two are significant at the 5 percent level. The magnitudes of the estimated elasticities of demand and

Table 7-4
Estimates of Price Elasticities: Oil-Gas Sample[a]

Plant[b]	E_{OO}	E_{OG}	E_{GO}	E_{GG}
1	−1.60	0.66	0.33	−0.36
2	−1.55	0.51	0.58	0.37
3	−1.55	0.52	0.53	0.25
4	−1.69	0.97	0.44	−0.18
5	−1.55	0.14	0.10	−0.61
6	−1.54	0.34	0.38	0.03
7	−1.80	1.34	0.59	0.11
8	−1.54	0.48	0.72	0.73
9	−1.72	1.06	0.45	−0.18
10	−2.03	1.98	0.85	0.63
11	−1.55	0.49	0.39	−0.08
12	−1.54	0.54	0.98	1.25
13	−1.56	0.51	0.33	−0.27
14	−1.54	0.41	0.56	0.41
15	−1.92	1.59	0.44	−0.29
16	−1.68	1.13	1.27	1.62
17	−1.56	0.32	0.13	−0.83
18	−1.54	0.46	0.95	1.26
19	−1.65	0.88	0.48	−0.06
20	−1.67	0.89	0.37	−0.34
21	−1.77	1.25	0.57	0.09
22	−1.67	1.05	0.89	0.84
23	−2.00	1.87	0.70	0.30
24	−1.61	0.63	0.27	−0.52
25	−1.59	0.66	0.43	−0.10
26	−1.56	0.63	0.69	0.55
27	−1.54	0.42	0.84	1.07
28	−1.75	1.18	0.53	−0.01
29	−1.55	0.26	0.31	−0.05
30	−1.57	0.66	0.76	0.69
31	−1.54	0.57	1.89	3.11
32	−1.63	0.82	0.47	−0.05
33	−1.62	0.98	2.65	4.40
34	−1.68	0.95	0.43	−0.21
35	−1.98	1.84	0.73	0.38
36	−1.55	0.46	1.57	2.56
37	−1.91	1.67	0.79	0.53
38	−1.64	0.93	0.72	0.49
39	−1.62	0.80	0.51	0.05
40	−1.55	0.57	0.83	0.91
41	−1.56	0.40	2.21	3.93
42	−1.57	0.68	0.85	0.88
43	−1.66	0.93	0.54	0.08
44	−1.84	1.63	2.99	4.96
45	−1.68	0.96	0.45	−0.16
46	−2.26	2.47	0.61	0.05
47	−1.74	1.28	1.11	1.25
48	−2.01	1.86	0.56	−0.02
49	−1.89	1.46	0.39	−0.41
50	−1.62	0.81	0.55	0.14
51	−1.65	0.91	0.54	0.08

Table 7-4 Continued

Plant[b]	E_{OO}	E_{OG}	E_{GO}	E_{GG}
52	−1.59	0.68	0.48	0.02
53	−1.65	0.91	0.54	0.08
54	−2.61	3.34	0.68	0.19
55	−1.55	0.60	1.05	1.35
56	−1.56	0.61	0.70	0.60
57	−3.48	5.29	0.58	−0.10
58	−1.55	0.55	0.67	0.55
59	−1.60	0.77	0.67	0.44
60	−1.58	0.67	0.60	0.31

[a]E_{ij} indicates the elasticity of demand for fuel i with respect to the price of fuel j.

[b]Listed in increasing order of size.

substitution are consistent with the hypothesis that fuels are substantially but not perfectly substitutable in existing electric power plants.

Tests of Hypotheses

The results of statistical tests of joint hypotheses concerning other characteristics of the production function are summarized in Table 7-7. An upper bound for the overall significance level for the group of tests is the sum of the individual significance levels. An overall significance level of .06 is assigned, and a significance level of .01 is allocated to each of the six chi-square tests of the joint hypotheses.[9] In performing the tests, the equality restrictions relating parameters in the profit and demand equations are imposed as maintained hypotheses.

As shown in Table 7-7, overall homotheticity, as well as group-wise homotheticity in fuels, is rejected for the coal-gas sample but accepted for the coal-oil and oil-gas samples. Homogeneity with respect to all inputs is also rejected for the coal-gas sample but accepted for the coal-oil and oil-gas samples.[10] The degree of homogeneity, and thus of returns to scale, for these samples can be computed as $\lambda + 1$; see Chapter 6. For the oil-gas sample, the computed degree of homogeneity is 1.10, and the standard error of λ is 0.04. Thus returns to scale are significantly greater than unity for this sample, but the extent of increasing returns is not very great.[11] The 95 percent confidence interval is 1.02 to 1.18. The degree of returns to scale in the coal-oil sample is 0.95, and the standard error of λ is 0.20.[12] Therefore, the estimated degree of returns to scale is not significantly greater than unity. However, the estimate is not very precise; the 95 percent confidence interval is 0.56 to 1.34.

Table 7-5
Estimates of Cross-Elasticities of Substitution: Electric Power Generation

Coal-Gas Sample		Coal-Oil Sample		Oil-Gas Sample			
Plant[a]	σ_{CG}	Plant[a]	σ_{CO}	Plant[a]	σ_{OG}	Plant[a]	σ_{OG}
1	−0.28	1	6.75	1	1.97	31	7.41
2	3.54	2	0.94	2	2.49	32	3.08
3	1.67	3	−0.56	3	2.37	33	16.52
4	1.07	4	11.24	4	3.32	34	3.19
5	−0.35	5	−6.03	5	0.34	35	9.01
6	0.28	6	15.37	6	1.33	36	5.14
7	0.93	7	1.22	7	5.57	37	8.83
8	−0.34	8	2.65	8	2.79	38	4.82
9	6.64	9	−20.02	9	3.65	39	3.19
10	2.37	10	1.78	10	11.04	40	3.65
11	0.01	11	3.98	11	1.81	41	6.22
12	0.81	12	−3.53	12	3.95	42	4.29
13	0.36	13	−61.33	13	1.64	43	3.81
14	0.28	14	−7.08	14	2.05	44	30.21
15	4.88	15	−7.01	15	5.03	45	3.33
16	−0.01	16	33.17	16	9.52	46	9.93
17	1.27	17	2.54	17	0.65	47	9.42
18	4.95			18	3.39	48	7.13
19	2.21			19	3.27	49	4.22
20	2.96			20	2.71	50	3.44
21	8.16			21	5.14	51	3.73
22	1107.95			22	6.49	52	2.39
23	2.31			23	8.73	53	3.71
24	1.92			24	1.66	54	14.63
25	0.09			25	2.39	55	4.59
26	8.57			26	3.36	56	3.35
27	4.35			27	2.87	57	19.26
28	3.35			28	4.55	58	2.97
29	5.16			29	0.98	59	3.87
30	−33.20			30	3.77	60	3.17
31	−46.85						

[a]Plants are listed in increasing order of size.

Lastly, the normalized restricted profit function is used to test for the existence and neutrality of embodied technical change. For the coal-oil sample, both absence and Hicksian neutrality of technical change are rejected. Absence of technical change is accepted for the coal-gas and oil-gas samples, but Hicksian neutrality of the profit function is accepted only for the oil-gas sample.

Concluding Comments

Estimation of a translog normalized restricted profit function provides estimates of elasticities of demand and substitution that are subject only to those a priori

Table 7-6
Elasticities of Demand and Substitution at Means of Data:
Electric Power Generation[a]

Price Elasticities of Demand[b]

Coal-Gas Sample		Coal-Oil Sample		Oil-Gas Sample	
E_{CC}	−0.43[c] (0.16)	E_{CC}	−1.15[c] (0.33)	E_{OO}	−1.60[c] (0.36)
E_{CG}	0.09 (0.47)	E_{CO}	0.99[c] (0.24)	E_{OG}	0.76[c] (0.24)
E_{GC}	0.45[c] (0.10)	E_{OC}	1.01[c] (0.24)	E_{GO}	0.58[c] (0.18)
E_{GG}	−1.43[c] (0.48)	E_{OO}	−1.50[c] (0.67)	E_{GG}	0.21 (0.23)

Cross-Elasticities of Substitution

Coal-Gas Sample		Coal-Oil Sample		Oil-Gas Sample	
σ_{GC}	1.50 (1.56)	σ_{CO}	4.06[c] (0.96)	σ_{OG}	3.36[c] (1.06)

[a]Evaluated at the means of the data. Figures in parentheses are approximate standard errors.
[b]E_{ij} indicates the elasticity of demand for fuel *i* with respect to the price of fuel *j*.
[c]Significant at the .05 level.

constraints implied by economic theory. In addition, this approach to modeling interfuel substitution makes it possible to test a number of hypotheses concerning other characteristics of the production process. The results indicate that steam electric power generation is characterized by substantial ex post interfuel substitution, homogeneity, absence of strong scale economies, and little embodied technical change.

These findings contradict some widely held beliefs about production of electric power and have potentially important implications for public policy. However, because of weaknesses in the data and in the performance of the model, further work is required to confirm the results. The translog normalized restricted profit function offers a fruitful approach for further research in this area.[13]

Notes

1. See Nordin (1947); Lomax (1952); Iulo (1961); Komiya (1962); Nerlove (1963); Barzel (1963, 1964); Dhrymes and Kurz (1964); Ling (1964); McFadden (1964); Galatin (1968); Belinfante (1969); Cowing (1970); Fuss

Table 7-7
Tests of Hypotheses: Electric Power Generation

	Number of Restrictions	Chi-Square Critical Value	Test Statistics		
			Coal-Gas	Coal-Oil	Oil-Gas
Homotheticity:					
All Inputs	2	9.2	16.2[b]	6.9	6.1
Fuels	1	6.6	14.1[b]	4.7	5.9
Homogeneity:					
All Inputs	3	11.3	26.5[b]	8.8	6.5
Fuels	4	13.3	40.3[b]	11.7	60.4[b]
Absence of Technical Change	6	16.8	16.0	29.5[b]	4.2
Hicksian Neutrality	4	13.3	15.3[b]	19.4[b]	3.4

[a]The level of significance for each test is .01.
[b]The null hypothesis is rejected.

(1970, 1971); Lawrence (1972); Joskow and Mishkin (1974); and Christensen and Greene (1976).

2. Fuss (1971) and Christensen and Greene (1976) are exceptions. Christensen and Greene estimate a translog unit cost function. The use of a cost function is appropriate only if utilities are cost minimizers. The extensive literature on the effects of regulation indicates that profit-maximizing regulated utilities will not minimize costs, see Averch and Johnson (1962) and Bailey (1973).

3. Fuss (1971) again is an exception. He tests putty-semiputty, putty-clay, and clay-clay hypotheses.

4. Estimation of the demand equations alone would not provide estimates of all the parameters appearing in the profit function. Under the more restrictive assumptions used in specifying the unit cost function estimated in Chapter 8, estimation of the demand equations does yield estimates of all the relevant parameters.

5. The effective number of available degrees of freedom is equal to the number of observations times the number of equations estimated.

6. The test statistics are 34.3 for the coal-gas sample, 257.1 for the coal-oil sample, and 18.4 for the oil-gas sample. The critical value is 26.2 at the .01 level and 32.9 at the .001 level.

7. Note that although there are only two variable inputs in the estimated profit functions, they need not be substitutes in the production of a variable output.

8. The estimated standard errors are computed by treating the ratio of normalized expenditure to normalized restricted profit as a parameter. Thus they are only rough approximations to the true standard error.

9. An alternative testing procedure would have been to perform Bonferroni t-tests on the joint hypotheses. However, Christensen (1973) has shown that the power of this test procedure is likely to be quite low.

10. This result conflicts with the conclusion of Nerlove (1963) that the production function may be homothetic but is not homogeneous. However, Nerlove's results were for firms rather than plants.

11. The extent of increasing returns is defined as the degree of homogeneity minus one.

12. For the coal-oil sample, the estimated degree of returns to scale for fuel inputs can also be computed and is equal to 0.73.

13. The translog normalized restricted profit function is used to obtain estimates of aggregate elasticities of demand and substitution for fuels in electric power generation in Atkinson and Halvorsen (1976b). Tests of efficiency in regulated utilities using a translog normalized unrestricted profit function are discussed in Atkinson and Halvorsen (1977).

8 Energy Substitution in Manufacturing

Introduction

Manufacturing industries account for approximately one-fourth the total energy consumed for power in the United States. Considerable shifts have occurred in the composition of the manufacturing sector's energy consumption in recent years. In 1971, electricity comprised 15.3 percent of total purchases of the four major types of energy, fuel oil 14.0 percent, gas 58.2 percent, and coal 12.5 percent. The shares in 1958 were electricity 11.9 percent, fuel oil 13.5 percent, gas 44.8 percent, and coal 29.8 percent. This chapter examines the extent to which shifts in the composition of energy consumption in manufacturing can be explained by changes in relative energy prices.

The characteristics of energy demand can be expected to vary across individual industries. Table 8-1 provides data on energy consumption by each two-digit manufacturing industry in 1974. Industry shares in total energy consumption in manufacturing range from 21.9 percent for industry 28, chemicals and allied products, to 0.2 percent for industry 21, tobacco manufacturers. Differences in energy consumption across industries are due to differences both in total output and in the energy intensiveness of production. Energy cost as a percent of value added is also shown in Table 8-1. By this measure, energy intensiveness varied from 12.7 percent for industry 29, petroleum and coal products, to 1.0 percent for industry 27, printing and publishing.

The apparent differences in energy consumption across industries indicate that the interrelationships between the demands for each type of energy should be examined on an industry-by-industry basis. Previous studies of industrial energy demand have generally considered the demand for only one type of energy, usually electric energy,[1] or have provided results only for total manufacturing rather than for individual industries.[2] In this chapter, complete systems of energy demand equations are estimated for each two-digit industry. Duality theory is used to derive the systems of demand equations from a translog unit cost function that imposes on the estimated elasticities of demand only those restrictions implied by economic theory.

The model is estimated with cross-section state data for 1971, 1962, and 1958. Results include estimates for each industry of own- and cross-price elasticities of demand for electricity, fuel oil, gas, and coal. The model performs well for industries accounting for most of the total consumption of energy in manufacturing in each year. The estimated elasticities indicate considerable variation in energy substitution both across industries and across types of energy. Aggregate manufacturing demand for energy appears to be highly price responsive. Estimated own-price elasticities for all types of energy except electricity are generally substantially greater than unity.

Estimation Procedures

The derivation of the model to be estimated is discussed in Chapter 6. The system of equations to be estimated for each industry is

$$M_E = \alpha_E + \gamma_{EO}(\ln P_O - \ln P_E) + \gamma_{EG}(\ln P_G - \ln P_E)$$
$$+ \gamma_{EC}(\ln P_C - \ln P_E) + u_E$$

$$M_O = \alpha_O + \gamma_{EO}(\ln P_E - \ln P_O) + \gamma_{OG}(\ln P_G - \ln P_O)$$
$$+ \gamma_{OC}(\ln P_C - \ln P_O) + u_O$$

$$M_G = \alpha_G + \gamma_{EG}(\ln P_E - \ln P_G) + \gamma_{OG}(\ln P_O - \ln P_G)$$
$$+ \gamma_{GC}(\ln P_C - \ln P_G) + u_G$$

(8.1)

where M_i is the cost share, and P_i is the price of the inputs, electricity, E, fuel oil, O, gas, G, and coal, C. For some industries there is an insufficient number of observations on the price of coal to estimate the full four-input model. For these industries, a three-input model is estimated. The system of equations estimated is,

$$M_E = \alpha_E + \gamma_{EO}(\ln P_O - \ln P_E) + \gamma_{EG}(\ln P_G - \ln P_E) + u_E$$
$$M_O = \alpha_O + \gamma_{EO}(\ln P_E - \ln P_O) + \gamma_{OG}(\ln P_G - \ln P_O) + u_O$$

(8.2)

For both models, the values of the parameters not included in the estimated equations can be computed using the adding-up restrictions:

$$\sum_i \alpha_i = 1 \qquad \sum_i \gamma_{ij} = 0$$

Alternatively, the values of all estimated parameters can be obtained directly by estimating additional combinations of the cost-share equations. For example, estimates of all parameters in the three-input model can be obtained directly by estimating the following sets of cost-share equations in addition to (8.2):

$$M_E = \alpha_E + \gamma_{EE}(\ln P_E - \ln P_G) + \gamma_{EO}(\ln P_O - \ln P_G) + u_E$$
$$M_O = \alpha_O + \gamma_{EO}(\ln P_E - \ln P_G) + \gamma_{OO}(\ln P_O - \ln P_G) + u_O$$

(8.3)

and

$$M_O = \alpha_O + \gamma_{OO}(\ln P_O - \ln P_E) + \gamma_{OG}(\ln P_G - \ln P_E) + u_E$$
$$M_G = \alpha_G + \gamma_{OG}(\ln P_O - \ln P_E) + \gamma_{GG}(\ln P_G - \ln P_E) + u_G$$

$$(8.4)$$

This approach has the advantage of providing direct estimates of the standard errors for all parameters.[3]

The systems of cost-share equations are estimated with *Census of Manufactures* data for 1971, 1962, and 1958. The census provides data on the quantity consumed and total cost for each type of energy.[4] The price of each type of energy is calculated by dividing cost by quantity consumed.[5]

Performance of the Model

The model including electricity, fuel oil, gas, and coal is estimated for 9 industries in 1971, 11 in 1962, and 8 in 1958. The industries for which the four-input

Table 8-1
Energy Consumption by Two-Digit Industries, 1974

Industry	Energy Consumption[a]	Percent of Total	Energy Intensiveness[b]
20 Food and Kindred Products	280.2	7.14%	3.22%
21 Tobacco Products	5.9	0.15	1.21
22 Textile Mill Products	94.5	2.41	5.24
23 Apparel, Other Textile Products	19.0	0.48	1.15
24 Lumber and Wood Products	79.6	2.03	4.17
25 Furniture and Fixtures	17.1	0.44	1.84
26 Paper and Allied Products	390.0	9.94	10.05
27 Printing and Publishing	26.5	0.68	1.03
28 Chemicals, Allied Products	858.1	21.86	7.71
29 Petroleum and Coal Products	459.4	11.70	12.68
30 Rubber, Misc. Plastic Products	74.7	1.90	3.63
31 Leather and Leather Products	6.7	0.17	1.70
32 Stone, Clay, and Glass Products	391.5	9.98	10.67
33 Primary Metal Industries	774.0	19.72	11.24
34 Fabricated Metal Products	120.7	3.08	2.33
35 Machinery, Except Electrical	107.8	2.75	1.48
36 Electrical Equipment and Supplies	73.5	1.87	1.64
37 Transportation Equipment	109.9	2.80	1.84
38 Instruments and Related Products	20.8	0.53	1.20
39 Miscellaneous Manufacturing Industries	15.0	0.38	1.68
Total	3924.7[c]	100.00%[c]	

Source: U.S. Bureau of the Census, *Annual Survey of Manufactures 1974.*
[a]Billions of kilowatt-hours equivalent.
[b]Energy cost as percent of value added.
[c]Detailed figures may not add to totals because of independent rounding.

model can be estimated tend to be the major energy users. For example, this group of industries accounted for 93.0 percent of coal purchases and 67.7 percent of total energy purchases in manufacturing in 1971. The model excluding coal is estimated for 10 industries in 1971, 4 in 1962, and 4 in 1958. There are too few observations to obtain results for the remaining two-digit industries in each year.

Derivation of the cost-share equations from the unit cost function implies cross-equation equality restrictions on the γ_{ij}; see Chapter 6. In order to test whether or not the loss of fit from imposing the equality restrictions is significant, the equations are estimated with and without the restrictions imposed. The results are compared by computing $-2 \log \lambda$, where λ is the ratio of the maximum value of the likelihood function for the restricted equations to the maximum value of the likelihood function for the unrestricted equations. Under the null hypothesis, this test statistic is distributed asymptotically as chi-squared with degrees of freedom equal to the number of restrictions being tested.

Test results are shown in Table 8-2. Because these restrictions are directly implied by derivation of the cost-share equations from the cost function, a very small significance level, .001, is used for the tests.[6] The cross-equation equality restrictions are rejected for three industries in 1971, three in 1962, and none in 1958.

Table 8-2
Tests of Cross-Equation Equality Restrictions: Manufacturing

	1971		1962		1958	
Industry	Test Statistic	Critical Value[a]	Test Statistic	Critical Value[a]	Test Statistic	Critical Value[a]
20	23.1[b]	22.4	24.0[b]	22.4	17.7	22.4
22	17.1[b]	16.3	19.7	22.4	19.5	22.4
23	11.1	16.3	5.3	16.3	N/E	–
24	4.0	16.3	9.4	16.3	6.7	16.3
25	13.7	16.3	13.9	22.4	N/E	–
26	4.1	22.4	7.4	22.4	21.7	22.4
27	1.0	16.3	12.6	16.3	N/E	–
28	4.9	22.4	18.5	22.4	13.6	16.3
29	11.3	16.3	8.6	16.3	N/E	–
30	17.0	22.4	27.9[b]	22.4	8.6	16.3
31	58.4[b]	16.3	N/E	–	N/E	–
32	10.5	22.4	10.5	22.4	15.1	22.4
33	12.4	22.4	14.3	22.4	4.4	16.3
34	21.7	22.4	54.9[b]	22.4	18.0	22.4
35	13.6	22.4	22.1	22.4	15.5	22.4
36	12.3	16.3	21.0	22.4	10.8	16.3
37	1.1	22.4	N/E	–	7.7	16.3
38	3.5	16.3	N/E	–	N/E	–
39	0.3	16.3	N/E	–	N/E	–

[a]Significance level is .001.
[b]The null hypothesis is rejected.
N/E means not estimated.

Tests of the separability of electricity, fuel oil, and gas from coal are performed for those industries for which the four-input model can be estimated. In every case, both weak separability of the true unit cost function and explicit separability of the translog approximation are accepted at the .01 level in all years.

Monotonicity of the unit cost function is checked by determining if the fitted values of the cost shares are positive. Of the 942 fitted cost shares in 1971, 938 are positive. Similarly, 700 of 713 are positive in 1962, and 579 of 584 are positive in 1958. Since it is not determined whether or not the negative fitted cost shares are significantly different from zero, this check does not provide a statistical test. However, a statistical test is available at the means of the data.

The price data are scaled such that the means of the prices are equal to unity. As a result, the logarithms of the means of the prices are equal to zero. Therefore, the fitted cost shares at the means of the data are equal to the estimated intercept terms, α_i. With the exception of α_G for industry 26 in 1958, which is positive but insignificant, all α_i are significantly positive in all years. Since the fitted cost shares are significantly positive, monotonicity is accepted at the means of the data.[7]

Concavity of the unit cost function is checked by examining the signs of the principal minors at each observation. The number of observations with principal minors of the incorrect sign are shown in Table 8-3. Although it is not deter-

Table 8-3
Signs of Principal Minors: Manufacturing

Number of Observations with Incorrect Signs

Industry	1971	1962	1958
20	24[a]	0	0
22	0	0	6[a]
23	0	0	N/E
24	10[a]	0	0
25	9[a]	0	N/E
26	0	2	0
27	10[a]	0	N/E
28	0	6[a]	0
29	0	0	N/E
30	0	10[a]	2
31	1	N/E	N/E
32	0	0	0
33	1	0	0
34	0	10[a]	1
35	0	0	0
36	0	0	0
37	9[a]	N/E	0
38	9[a]	N/E	N/E
39	3[a]	N/E	N/E

[a]The concavity condition is considered to be violated for this industry.
N/E means not estimated.

mined if the principal minors with incorrect signs are statistically significant, the existence of incorrect signs for more than a few percent of the observations is considered to indicate that the concavity condition is violated for the industry in question.[8]

The performance of the model is questionable with respect to either the regularity conditions or cross-equation equality restrictions for nine industries in 1971, four in 1962, and two in 1958. However, the model performs very well for the remaining industries in each year. The industries for which the model performs well account for most of the manufacturing sector's consumption of energy in each year. For example, the group of industries for which the model performed well accounted for 81.6 percent of total energy purchases in manufacturing in 1971. The share of this group in the purchases of each type of energy in 1971 was 76.1 percent for electricity, 78.0 percent for fuel oil, 85.7 percent for gas, and 87.6 percent for coal. For brevity, further results are discussed only for the industries for which the model performs well.[9]

Parameter Estimates

Estimates of the parameters and their asymptotic standard errors are shown in Tables 8-4, 8-5, and 8-6, together with the value of the "pseudo-R^2" for each system of equations.[10]   The pseudo-R^2 states the proportion of generalized variance in the system of equations explained by variation in the righthand variables. It is calculated as $1 - |r_1|/|r_2|$, where $|r_1|$ is the determinant of the estimated residual moment matrix, and $|r_2|$ is the determinant when the coefficients of all righthand variables are constrained to equal zero. The value of the pseudo-R^2 is invariant to the choice of equation to be omitted from the system (Berndt 1977).

The estimated parameters have direct economic interpretations. From equation (6.18), estimates of the elasticity of the unit cost of energy with respect to the price of energy input i, $\partial \ln V/\partial \ln P_i$, are equal to the fitted cost shares of energy input i. The estimated α_i are equal to the fitted cost shares at the means of the data and therefore indicate the responsiveness of the unit cost of aggregate energy to the prices of each type of energy at the means of the data. As shown in Tables 8-4 through 8-6, the unit cost of aggregate energy is most responsive to the price of electricity. The average values of the estimated α_i parameters in 1971 are, $\alpha_E = 0.58$, $\alpha_O = 0.11$, $\alpha_G = 0.24$, and $\alpha_C = 0.10$.

The estimates of the γ_{ij} parameters can be interpreted as estimated share elasticities. The cost share of input i is equal to $\partial \ln V/\partial \ln P_i$. The cross-partial derivative

$$\frac{\partial^2 \ln V}{\partial \ln P_i \partial \ln P_j} = \gamma_{ij}$$

can be defined as a constant share elasticity summarizing the response of cost share M_i to a change in $\ln P_j$. Alternatively, the share elasticity can be defined as

$$\frac{\partial \ln M_i}{\partial \ln P_j} = \frac{\gamma_{ij}}{M_i}$$

In the latter case, the estimated share elasticities at the means of data will be equal to the estimates of γ_{ij}/α_i.

Elasticity Estimates

Because the elasticities of demand are functions of the cost shares, they will vary across the sample.[11] Rather than report the estimated elasticities for each observation, the elasticities are evaluated at the means of the data, and only these values are reported here.[12] Since the estimated α_k, $k = E, O, G, C$, are equal to the fitted cost shares at the means of the data, the formulas for the elasticities of demand at the means are given by equations (6.25) and (6.26), with M_k replaced by α_k:

$$E_{ii} = \frac{\alpha_i^2 - \alpha_i + \gamma_{ii}}{\alpha_i} \quad i = E, O, G, C \tag{8.5}$$

$$E_{ij} = \frac{\alpha_i\alpha_j + \gamma_{ij}}{\alpha_i} \quad i, j = E, O, G, C \tag{8.6}$$

Because the elasticities at the means are functions only of the estimated parameters, the calculation of their estimated standard errors is considerably simplified. A first-order Taylor series approximation to the variance of the estimated elasticities can be computed as

$$S_B{}'V(B)S_B \tag{8.7}$$

where S_B is the column vector of first partial derivatives of the elasticities with respect to the parameters α_k and γ_{km} and $V(B)$ is the estimated variance-covariance matrix of the parameter estimates (Kmenta 1971, pp. 443-444).

Estimates of the own- and cross-price elasticities of demand at the means of the data are shown in Tables 8-7, 8-8, and 8-9, together with their asymptotic standard errors. Because the elasticities are derived from unit cost functions for energy, they show the price responsiveness of demand for individual types of energy holding total energy input constant.

Estimates of the own-price elasticities are shown in the first four rows of the tables. All the own-price elasticities have the correct sign in all years. For 1971,

Table 8–4
Estimates of Parameters of the Cost Function, 1971[a]

Parameter	Industry									
	23	26	28	29	30	32	33	34	35	36
α_E	.856b (.017)	.414b (.022)	.518b (.021)	.371b (.041)	.683b (.018)	.354b (.013)	.561b (.020)	.662b (.014)	.668b (.008)	.744b (.012)
α_O	.065b (.009)	.206b (.031)	.107b (.106)	.175b (.034)	.093b (.016)	.083b (.015)	.120b (.021)	.078b (.026)	.061b (.008)	.078b (.011)
α_G	.079b (.013)	.200b (.023)	.210b (.020)	.454b (.050)	.162b (.013)	.390b (.024)	.269b (.020)	.232b (.019)	.230b (.009)	.178b (.016)
α_C	N/E	.181b (.029)	.165b (.025)	N/E	.062b (.016)	.173b (.022)	.050b (.013)	.027b (.006)	.041b (.005)	N/E
γ_{EE}	-.033 (.077)	.158 (.127)	-.104 (.087)	-.149 (.116)	.132 (.111)	.118 (.091)	-.219b (.073)	-.503b (.238)	-.308b (.074)	-.012 (.055)
γ_{EO}	.073 (.044)	-.006 (.113)	.161b (.058)	.174 (.092)	-.120b (.061)	-.061 (.056)	.098 (.054)	.231b (.133)	.088 (.063)	.001 (.033)
γ_{EG}	-.070 (.052)	-.093 (.081)	.048 (.063)	-.024 (.080)	-.037 (.087)	-.018 (.064)	.100 (.059)	.191 (.148)	.153b (.045)	.011 (.048)
γ_{EC}	N/E	-.060 (.079)	-.105 (.074)	N/E	.025 (.065)	-.040 (.081)	.020 (.042)	.079 (.067)	.067b (.022)	N/E
γ_{OO}	-.104b (.040)	-.302b (.148)	-.282b (.077)	-.228b (.095)	-.022 (.078)	-.214b (.072)	-.224b (.076)	-.248 (.179)	-.204b (.069)	-.074b (.035)
γ_{OG}	.031 (.028)	.206 (.148)	.123b (.058)	.055 (.064)	.101 (.060)	.146b (.070)	.036 (.063)	.018 (.127)	.081 (.045)	.073b (.037)
γ_{OC}	N/E	.103 (.087)	-.002 (.064)	N/E	.041 (.053)	.129 (.073)	.090b (.041)	-.002 (.052)	.035 (.022)	N/E

γ_{GG}	.040 (.046)	-.266[b] (.098)	-.248[b] (.083)	-.030 (.098)	-.098 (.084)	-.280[b] (.123)	-.056 (.079)	-.160 (.156)	-.173[b] (.049)	-.083 (.062)
γ_{GC}	N/E	.153[b] (.076)	.077 (.070)	N/E	.033 (.046)	.153 (.100)	-.081[b] (.040)	-.049 (.041)	-.060[b] (.019)	N/E
γ_{CC}	N/E	-.197[b] (.101)	.030 (.106)	N/E	-.099 (.060)	-.242 (.136)	-.029 (.043)	-.028 (.027)	-.041[b] (.013)	N/E
Number of Observations	13	18	23	17	9	18	15	8	9	24
Pseudo-R^2	.309	.603	.565	.216	.799	.539	.638	.413	.912	.184

[a]Figures in parentheses are asymptotic standard errors.
[b]Significant at the .05 level.
N/E means not estimated.

Table 8-5
Estimates of Parameters of the Cost Function, 1962[a]

						Industry					
Parameter	22	23	24	25	26	27	29	32	33	35	36
α_E	.635[b] (.022)	.787[b] (.026)	.677[b] (.020)	.657[b] (.017)	.377[b] (.032)	.784[b] (.010)	.295[b] (.082)	.318[b] (.015)	.478[b] (.023)	.593[b] (.022)	.689[b] (.008)
α_O	.170[b] (.047)	.123[b] (.022)	.220[b] (.025)	.106[b] (.017)	.254[b] (.037)	.089[b] (.014)	.232[b] (.082)	.092[b] (.023)	.173[b] (.029)	.168[b] (.027)	.139[b] (.016)
α_G	.085[b] (.026)	.090[b] (.020)	.103[b] (.021)	.108[b] (.024)	.053 (.045)	.127[b] (.020)	.474[b] (.048)	.393[b] (.044)	.286[b] (.018)	.157[b] (.022)	.124[b] (.014)
α_C	.110[b] (.035)	N/E	N/E	.129[b] (.015)	.316[b] (.059)	N/E	N/E	.197[b] (.030)	.062[b] (.010)	.082[b] (.017)	.048[b] (.010)
γ_{EE}	−.032 (.044)	−.025 (.133)	−.074 (.067)	−.952[b] (.330)	.062 (.082)	.074 (.040)	−.514 (.309)	.096 (.052)	−.202[b] (.043)	−.184[b] (.068)	−.306[b] (.013)
γ_{EO}	.007 (.008)	.009 (.013)	−.045[b] (.013)	.049[b] (.015)	.002 (.012)	.004 (.010)	−.047 (.027)	.003 (.009)	−.018 (.110)	−.020 (.014)	.011 (.006)
γ_{EG}	−.055 (.040)	.024 (.135)	.118 (.075)	.937[b] (.349)	.031 (.080)	−.078[b] (.036)	.647[b] (.116)	−.074 (.050)	.178[b] (.032)	.073 (.049)	.146[b] (.025)
γ_{EC}	.081 (.046)	N/E	N/E	−.034 (.069)	−.094 (.076)	N/E	N/E	−.025 (.049)	.042[b] (.019)	.131[b] (.056)	.149[b] (.021)
γ_{OO}	.019 (.015)	.013 (.011)	.053[b] (.015)	.016 (.013)	.044[b] (.012)	−.011 (.013)	.030 (.026)	.011 (.014)	.010 (.013)	.022 (.016)	.034[b] (.011)
γ_{OG}	−.020[b] (.009)	−.014 (.010)	−.008 (.014)	−.056[b] (.020)	−.031 (.017)	.007 (.017)	.018 (.019)	−.026 (.026)	.003 (.008)	−.008 (.014)	−.023[b] (.011)
γ_{OC}	−.006 (.011)	N/E	N/E	−.009 (.011)	−.016 (.020)	N/E	N/E	.012 (.018)	.005 (.004)	.005 (.011)	−.023[b] (.007)

γ_{GG}	.025 (.064)	−.010 (.138)	−.110 (.084)	−.926[b] (.389)	−.177 (.120)	.071 (.039)	−.666[b] (.130)	−.182 (.132)	−.178[b] (.028)	−.001 (.059)	−.138 (.085)
γ_{GC}	.051 (.065)	N/E	N/E	.038 (.095)	.177 (.103)	N/E	N/E	.282[b] (.104)	−.004 (.014)	−.066 (.047)	.014 (.060)
γ_{CC}	−.125 (.086)	N/E	N/E	.004 (.047)	−.067 (.133)	N/E	N/E	−.269[b] (.100)	−.043[b] (.019)	−.070 (.067)	−.141 (.047)
Number of Observations	11	10	11	8	18	9	9	17	14	13	9
Pseudo-R^2	.64	.21	.62	.65	.70	.31	.80	.53	.81	.34	.99

[a]Figures in parentheses are asymptotic standard errors.
[b]Significant at the .05 level.
N/E means not estimated.

Table 8–6
Estimates of Parameters of the Cost Function, 1958[a]

Parameter	Industry									
	20	24	26	28	32	33	34	35	36	37
α_E	.498[b] (.015)	.729[b] (.028)	.333[b] (.025)	.632[b] (.024)	.314[b] (.010)	.550[b] (.023)	.646[b] (.012)	.707[b] (.036)	.813[b] (.016)	.724[b] (.025)
α_O	.162[b] (.016)	.165[b] (.031)	.138[b] (.044)	.143[b] (.018)	.149[b] (.025)	.234[b] (.030)	.146[b] (.014)	.081[b] (.010)	.090[b] (.009)	.149[b] (.029)
α_G	.190[b] (.016)	.106[b] (.014)	.047[b] (.012)	.225[b] (.024)	.282[b] (.039)	.217[b] (.021)	.145[b] (.013)	.109[b] (.011)	.097[b] (.011)	.127[b] (.008)
α_C	.150[b] (.017)	N/E	.483[b] (.053)	N/E	.255[b] (.023)	N/E	.062[b] (.008)	.103[b] (.024)	N/E	N/E
γ_{EE}	-.062 (.058)	-.119[b] (.036)	-.057 (.063)	-.153[b] (.049)	-.037 (.031)	-.227[b] (.048)	.087 (.073)	-.135 (.210)	-.160 (.110)	-.114 (.081)
γ_{EO}	.071 (.058)	-.015 (.021)	.036 (.057)	.067[b] (.029)	.054[b] (.021)	.115[b] (.050)	-.032 (.043)	-.029 (.072)	.127[b] (.060)	.070 (.075)
γ_{EG}	-.018 (.045)	.134[b] (.032)	.094[b] (.026)	.106[b] (.044)	.063 (.034)	.112[b] (.041)	-.042 (.320)	.127[b] (.062)	.033 (.068)	.043 (.040)
γ_{EC}	.009 (.040)	N/E	-.074 (.063)	N/E	-.079[b] (.033)	N/E	-.013 (.457)	.037 (.114)	N/E	N/E
γ_{OO}	-.261[b] (.048)	.001 (.024)	-.061 (.091)	-.213[b] (.018)	-.001 (.056)	-.179[b] (.078)	.075 (.051)	-.013 (.036)	-.185[b] (.043)	-.126 (.086)
γ_{OG}	.103[b] (.042)	.014 (.010)	-.003 (.029)	.146[b] (.047)	-.085 (.067)	.064 (.062)	-.041 (.372)	.050[b] (.024)	.058 (.033)	.056[b] (.023)
γ_{OC}	.086[b] (.037)	N/E	.029 (.095)	N/E	.033 (.051)	N/E	-.003 (.030)	-.009 (.032)	N/E	N/E

γ_{GG}	-.096 (.061)	-.148[b] (.034)	-.105[b] (.024)	-.252[b] (.067)	-.211 (.123)	-.176[b] (.072)	.061 (.036)	-.259[b] (.029)	-.091 (.051)	-.099[b] (.030)
γ_{GC}	.011 (.039)	N/E	.014 (.028)	N/E	.234[b] (.080)	N/E	.023 (.022)	.082[b] (.033)	N/E	N/E
γ_{CC}	-.106[b] (.048)	N/E	.032 (.120)	N/E	-.187[b] (.091)	N/E	-.007 (.038)	-.110 (.077)	N/E	N/E
Number of Observations	29	7	10	22	17	20	11	8	11	13
Pseudo-R²	.56	.72	.83	.69	.53	.57	.33	.94	.74	.61

[a]Figures in parentheses are asymptotic standard errors.
[b]Significant at the .05 level.
N/E means not estimated.

Table 8-7
Estimates of Price Elasticities: Manufacturing, 1971[a]

Elasticity	Industry									
	23	26	28	29	30	32	33	34	35	36
E_{EE}	-.148[b] (.090)	-.203 (.307)	-.684[b] (.171)	-1.031[b] (.317)	-.124 (.162)	-.312 (.257)	-.829[b] (.136)	-1.096[b] (.358)	-.793[b] (.112)	-.272[b] (.075)
E_{OO}	-2.528[b] (.658)	-2.262[b] (.759)	-3.513[b] (.791)	-2.132[b] (.610)	-1.151 (.835)	-3.497[b] (.986)	-2.748[b] (.671)	-4.113 (2.510)	-4.300[b] (1.181)	-1.870[b] (.468)
E_{GG}	-.425 (.582)	-2.134[b] (.519)	-1.972[b] (.421)	-.613[b] (.213)	-1.439[b] (.522)	-1.329[b] (.326)	-.936[b] (.297)	-1.457[b] (.678)	-1.522[b] (.218)	-1.292[b] (.355)
E_{CC}	N/E	-1.907[b] (.601)	-.656 (.640)	N/E	-2.531[b] (1.092)	-2.223[b] (.811)	-1.529[b] (.895)	-2.004[b] (1.041)	-1.968[b] (.350)	N/E
E_{EO}	.150[b] (.053)	.191 (.273)	.418[b] (.116)	.643[b] (.252)	-.082 (.091)	-.088 (.159)	.295[b] (.102)	.428[b] (.202)	.193[b] (.096)	.079 (.045)
E_{EG}	-.003 (.061)	-.024 (.198)	.303[b] (.124)	.388 (.214)	.109 (.127)	.340 (.182)	.449[b] (.108)	.520[b] (.224)	.460[b] (.068)	.192[b] (.067)
E_{EC}	N/E	.037 (.190)	-.037 (.144)	N/E	.979[b] (.096)	.060 (.230)	.086 (.076)	.147 (.101)	.141[b] (.033)	N/E
E_{OE}	1.976[b] (.717)	.383 (.546)	2.015[b] (.577)	1.364[b] (.573)	-.608 (.693)	-.377 (.687)	1.379[b] (.470)	3.645 (1.984)	2.123[b] (1.053)	.758 (.420)
E_{OG}	.552 (.433)	1.198[b] (.518)	1.350[b] (.561)	.766[b] (.366)	1.255 (.669)	2.143[b] (.902)	.571 (.518)	.469 (1.626)	1.560[b] (.757)	1.111[b] (.499)
E_{OC}	N/E	.680 (.428)	.148 (.592)	N/E	.504 (.568)	1.731 (.919)	.798[b] (.354)	-.001 (.667)	.617 (.356)	N/E
E_{GE}	-.029 (.665)	-.050 (.410)	.748[b] (.302)	.318 (.183)	.458 (.532)	.309 (.165)	.933[b] (.224)	1.483[b] (.644)	1.333[b] (.197)	.804[b] (.272)

E_{GO}	.454 (.362)	1.237b (.526)	.691b (.289)	.295 (.151)	.716 (.382)	.456b (.184)	.254 (.237)	.157 (.547)	.411 (.218)	.488b (.214)
E_{GC}	N/E	.948b (.386)	.533 (.339)	N/E	.265 (.284)	.564b (.260)	-.251 (.154)	-.183 (.178)	-.221b (.084)	N/E
E_{CE}	N/E	.084 (.434)	-.117 (.454)	N/E	1.081 (1.068)	.124 (.471)	.966 (.854)	3.554 (2.585)	2.298b (.580)	N/E
E_{CO}	N/E	.775 (.492)	.096 (.386)	N/E	.754 (.884)	.829 (.432)	1.922 (.996)	-.004 (1.891)	.912 (.555)	N/E
E_{CG}	N/E	1.047b (.440)	.676 (.430)	N/E	.695 (.749)	1.270b (.590)	-1.359 (.934)	-1.546 (1.552)	-1.242b (.507)	N/E

[a]Figures in parentheses are asymptotic standard errors.
[b]Significant at the .05 level.
N/E means not estimated.

114

Table 8-8
Estimates of Price Elasticities: Manufacturing, 1962[a]

| Elasticity | \multicolumn{11}{c}{Industry} | | | | | | | | | | |
	22	23	24	25	26	27	29	32	33	35	36
E_{EE}	-.416[b] (.076)	-.245 (.172)	-.432[b] (.109)	-1.793[b] (.492)	-.459[b] (.223)	-.121[b] (.049)	-2.738[b] (.791)	-.380[b] (.162)	-.944[b] (.091)	-.719[b] (.124)	-.756[b] (.022)
E_{OO}	-.718[b] (.103)	-.769[b] (.094)	-.538[b] (.066)	-.746[b] (.122)	-.571[b] (.057)	-1.030[b] (.156)	-.641[b] (.139)	-.788[b] (.143)	-.770[b] (.090)	-.699[b] (.097)	-.615[b] (.076)
E_{GG}	-.625 (.762)	-1.022 (1.524)	-1.966[b] (.741)	-9.418[b] (4.309)	-4.303[b] (2.446)	-.314 (.314)	-1.931[b] (.212)	-1.069[b] (.327)	-1.334[b] (.117)	-.845[b] (.365)	-1.986[b] (.684)
E_{CC}	-2.024[b] (.805)	N/E	N/E	-.843[b] (.360)	-.895[b] (.450)	N/E	N/E	-2.171[b] (.557)	-1.634[b] (.302)	-1.764[b] (.833)	-3.890[b] (1.200)
E_{EO}	.181[b] (.043)	.124[b] (.023)	.154[b] (.028)	.180[b] (.028)	.259[b] (.048)	.094[b] (.020)	.071 (.099)	.102[b] (.040)	.135[b] (.030)	.135[b] (.032)	.156[b] (.015)
E_{EG}	-.002 (.069)	.120 (.175)	.278[b] (.122)	1.535[b] (.524)	.134 (.230)	.028 (.048)	2.667[b] (.845)	.161 (.166)	.658[b] (.068)	.282[b] (.090)	.336[b] (.040)
E_{EC}	.237[b] (.084)	N/E	N/E	.078 (.105)	.066 (.208)	N/E	N/E	.118 (.161)	.151[b] (.040)	.303[b] (.099)	.264[b] (.031)
E_{OE}	.677[b] (.067)	.794[b] (.126)	.473[b] (.070)	1.113[b] (.176)	.384[b] (.076)	.826[b] (.118)	.091 (.144)	.352[b] (.108)	.373[b] (.072)	.476[b] (.093)	.771[b] (.051)
E_{OG}	-.035 (.064)	-.025 (.099)	.065 (.079)	-.415[b] (.210)	-.068 (.107)	.204 (.201)	.550[b] (.132)	.107 (.290)	.305[b] (.059)	.112 (.096)	-.039 (.084)
E_{OC}	.076 (.090)	N/E	N/E	.047 (.110)	.255[b] (.127)	N/E	N/E	.328 (.219)	.092[b] (.035)	.111 (.075)	-.116[b] (.060)
E_{GE}	-.015 (.520)	1.056 (1.498)	1.826[b] (.663)	9.340[b] (4.024)	.960 (1.461)	.171 (.291)	1.662[b] (.197)	.130 (.128)	1.100[b] (.130)	1.061[b] (.306)	1.867[b] (.242)

E_{GO}	-.069 (.144)	-.035 (.140)	.140 (.147)	-.409 (.254)	-.326 (.781)	.143 (.132)	.269^b (.008)	.025 (.065)	.184^b (.036)	.120 (.087)	-.044 (.097)
E_{GC}	.709 (.816)	N/E	N/E	.486 (1.885)	3.669 (2.848)	N/E	N/E	.914^b (.273)	.049 (.051)	-.335 (.304)	.164 (.482)
E_{CE}	1.364^b (.456)	N/E	N/E	.396 (.534)	.078 (.246)	N/E	N/E	.191 (.251)	1.155^b (.316)	2.178^b (.729)	3.804^b (.801)
E_{CO}	.117 (.104)	N/E	N/E	.039 (.088)	.205^b (.070)	N/E	N/E	.153 (.089)	.254^b (.060)	.226 (.124)	-.340 (.221)
E_{CG}	.543 (.592)	N/E	N/E	.408 (.732)	.612 (.397)	N/E	N/E	1.827^b (.616)	.225 (.228)	-.640 (.553)	.425 (1.267)

[a]Figures in parentheses are asymptotic standard errors.
[b]Significant at the .05 level.
N/E means not estimated.

Table 8-9
Estimates of Price Elasticities: Manufacturing, 1958[a]

Elasticity	Industry									
	20	24	26	28	32	33	34	35	36	37
E_{EE}	-.626[b] (.116)	-.435[b] (.051)	-.837[b] (.190)	-.641[b] (.081)	-.804[b] (.098)	-.864[b] (.103)	-.219[b] (.112)	-.484[b] (.291)	-.383[b] (.135)	-.433[b] (.112)
E_{OO}	-2.449[b] (.342)	-.827[b] (.162)	-1.308[b] (.693)	-2.345[b] (.373)	-.861[b] (.365)	-1.534[b] (.345)	-.336 (.358)	-1.075[b] (.463)	-2.979[b] (.527)	-1.699[b] (.631)
E_{GG}	-1.316[b] (.324)	-2.288[b] (.359)	-3.189[b] (.761)	-1.895[b] (.322)	-1.466[b] (.455)	-1.598[b] (.341)	-.441[b] (.244)	-3.266[b] (.368)	-1.841[b] (.543)	-1.651[b] (.247)
E_{CC}	-1.554[b] (.347)	N/E	-.452[b] (.254)	N/E	-1.480[b] (.365)	N/E	-1.054[b] (.601)	-1.967[b] (.822)	N/E	N/E
E_{EO}	.304[b] (.079)	.144[b] (.030)	.246 (.173)	.249[b] (.053)	.320[b] (.072)	.443[b] (.103)	.097 (.067)	.309[b] (.100)	.246[b] (.074)	.246[b] (.106)
E_{EG}	.154 (.091)	.290[b] (.046)	.331[b] (.083)	.393[b] (.079)	.482[b] (.120)	.420[b] (.082)	.080 (.050)	.289[b] (.086)	.138 (.084)	.187[b] (.054)
E_{EC}	.168[b] (.080)	N/E	.261 (.192)	N/E	.002 (.108)	N/E	.042 (.070)	.155 (.159)	N/E	N/E
E_{OE}	.938[b] (.235)	.639[b] (.134)	.594 (.427)	1.099[b] (.210)	.674[b] (.150)	1.042[b] (.217)	.429 (.293)	.347 (.893)	2.230[b] (.688)	1.798[b] (.530)
E_{OG}	.828[b] (.267)	.188[b] (.078)	.022 (.214)	1.246[b] (.363)	-.290 (.450)	.492 (.268)	-.136 (.258)	.734[b] (.288)	.749[b] (.365)	.501[b] (.181)
E_{OC}	.623[b] (.229)	N/E	.692 (.703)	N/E	.476 (.345)	N/E	.042 (.202)	-.005 (.394)	N/E	N/E
E_{GE}	.403 (.238)	1.996[b] (.354)	2.353[b] (.778)	1.102[b] (.200)	.536[b] (.125)	1.066[b] (.192)	.356 (.220)	1.874[b] (.610)	1.151 (.706)	1.065[b] (.317)

E_{GO}	.705[b] (.228)	.292[b] (.091)	.064 (.629)	.793[b] (.223)	-.153 (.240)	.531 (.291)	-.136 (.255)	.542[b] (.213)	.690[b] (.340)	.587[b] (.189)
E_{GC}	.208 (.204)	N/E	.771 (.581)	N/E	1.083[b] (.307)	N/E	.221 (.152)	.850[b] (.301)	N/E	N/E
E_{CE}	.557[b] (.267)	N/E	.180 (.131)	N/E	.002 (.132)	N/E	.438 (.731)	1.068 (1.131)	N/E	N/E
E_{CO}	.735[b] (.258)	N/E	.197 (.203)	N/E	.278 (.198)	N/E	.099 (.492)	-.004 (.309)	N/E	N/E
E_{CG}	.263 (.258)	N/E	.075 (.058)	N/E	1.199[b] (.334)	N/E	.517 (.351)	.903[b] (.352)	N/E	N/E

[a]Figures in parentheses are asymptotic standard errors.
[b]Significant at the .05 level.
N/E means not estimated.

30 of the 37 estimates are significant at the 5 percent level using one-tailed tests. For 1962, 36 of 40 are significant, and for 1958, 34 of 35 are significant. There is considerable variation across industries in the estimated own-price elasticities. For example, in 1971 the range is −0.12 to −1.10 for electricity, −1.15 to −4.30 for fuel oil, −0.42 to −2.13 for gas, and −0.66 to −2.53 for coal.

The estimates of the cross-price elasticities also show considerable variation across industries. The relationship between different types of energy appears to be predominantly that of substitutes rather than complements. In 1971, only 18 of the 102 estimates are negative, and only 2 of the negative estimates are statistically significant at the 5 percent level using two-tailed tests. In 1962, 16 of 108 estimated cross-elasticities are negative, of which 2 are significant. In 1958, 6 of 90 estimated cross-elasticities are negative, and none of the negative estimates are statistically significant.

As would be expected, the estimates of the cross-price elasticities tend to be smaller in absolute magnitude than the estimates of own-price elastiticites.[13] However, the results do indicate significant cross-price responsiveness of energy demand. In 1971, 39 of the 84 positive estimates are significant at the 5 percent level.[14] Similarly, 50 of the 92 positive estimates are significant in 1962, and 48 of 84 are significant in 1958.

The estimated parameters are also used to obtain estimates of Allen cross-partial elasticities of substitution. As discussed in Chapter 6, the Allen elasticities can be interpreted as normalized price elasticities where the normalization is chosen such that the cross-elasticities of substitution are invariant to the ordering of the inputs. From equation (6.27), the estimated Allen cross-elasticities at the means of the data are computed as

$$\sigma_{ij} = \frac{1}{\alpha_j} E_{ij} = \frac{\alpha_i \alpha_j + \gamma_{ij}}{\alpha_i \alpha_j}$$

Approximate asymptotic standard errors of the estimated elasticities of substitution at the means of the data can be obtained using equation (8.7).

Estimates of the Allen cross-elasticities of substitution for each industry in 1971 are shown in Table 8-10. The signs of the cross-elasticities of substitution are equal to the signs of the cross-price elasticities. Of the 51 estimated cross-elasticities of substitution, 20 are significant at the 5 percent level, of which only 1 is negative.

Aggregate price elasticities for the group of industries for which the model performed well in each year are estimated by constructing weighted averages for individual industries. The weights are each industry's share of total group purchases for the relevant type of energy.[15] Since the model performs well for industries accounting for most of the energy consumed in manufacturing in each year, the group elasticities provide reasonable approximations to the aggregate elasticities for total manufacturing.

Table 8-10
Estimates of Allen Cross-Elasticities of Substitution: Manufacturing, 1971[a]

	Industry									
	23	26	28	29	30	32	33	34	35	36
σ_{EO}	2.308b (.830)	.927 (1.319)	3.894b (1.117)	3.680b (1.546)	-.890 (1.016)	-1.064 (1.942)	2.459b (.839)	5.488 (2.968)	3.177b (1.581)	1.019 (.564)
σ_{EG}	-.034 (.777)	-.122 (.991)	1.446b (.581)	.855 (.471)	.670 (.779)	.872 (.466)	1.664b (.392)	2.239b (.969)	1.995b (.293)	1.080b (.365)
σ_{EC}	N/E	.203 (1.050)	-.226 (.877)	N/E	1.582 (1.558)	.349 (1.329)	1.723 (1.518)	5.367 (3.893)	3.440b (.854)	N/E
σ_{OG}	6.980 (5.574)	6.003b (2.515)	6.436b (2.723)	1.687b (.797)	7.736 (4.053)	5.496b (2.268)	2.119 (1.933)	2.020 (6.998)	6.774b (3.273)	6.252b (2.739)
σ_{OC}	N/E	3.764 (2.379)	.898 (3.588)	N/E	8.151 (9.374)	9.992 (5.385)	16.019 (8.225)	-.051 (24.293)	15.044 (8.793)	N/E
σ_{GC}	N/E	5.244b (2.202)	3.223 (2.040)	N/E	4.285 (4.627)	3.258b (1.496)	-5.041 (3.513)	-6.652 (6.837)	-5.391b (2.277)	N/E

[a]Figures in parentheses are asymptotic standard errors.
[b]Significant at the .05 level.
N/E means not estimated.

The weighted average elasticities are shown in Table 8-11. With the exception of oil, the estimated own-price elasticities are fairly consistent in each of the three years. The oil own-price elasticity is much larger in absolute magnitude in 1971 than in the earlier years. The cross-price elasticities of demand for oil with respect to the prices of other types of energy are also considerably larger in 1971 than in earlier years.

Price elasticities estimated with a unit cost function for energy show the extent of price responsiveness holding aggregate energy input constant. As discussed in Chapter 6, estimated elasticities of demand incorporating the effects of price changes on aggregate energy input can be computed as

$$E_{ij}^T = E_{ij} + E_{HV}M_j \quad i, j = E, O, G, C \quad (8.8)$$

where E_{ij} is the price elasticity estimated with a unit cost function for energy, and E_{HV} is the elasticity of demand for aggregate energy with respect to the price of aggregate energy.

Berndt and Wood (1975) obtained estimates for E_{HV} for each year for total U.S. manufacturing. Their estimates are substituted in equation (8.8) to obtain estimates of the elasticities of demand for each type of energy allowing total energy input to vary. The weighted average elasticities for the group of industries are shown in Table 8-12.[16]

Table 8-11
Estimates of Aggregate Manufacturing Price Elasticities:
Total Energy Input Constant

Elasticity	1971	1962	1958
E_{EE}	−.66	−.87	−.67
E_{OO}	−2.75	−.70	−1.63
E_{GG}	−1.32	−1.75	−1.76
E_{CC}	−1.46	−1.62	−1.51
E_{EO}	.30	.14	.33
E_{EG}	.34	.59	.35
E_{EC}	.09	.13	.03
E_{OE}	1.27	.41	.89
E_{OG}	1.12	.15	.46
E_{OC}	.69	.14	.40
E_{GE}	.43	.95	1.01
E_{GO}	.50	.12	.42
E_{GC}	.32	.53	.32
E_{CE}	.31	.71	.30
E_{CO}	.74	.18	.42
E_{CG}	.40	.72	.79

Table 8-12
Estimates of Aggregate Manufacturing Price Elasticities:
Total Energy Input Variable

Elasticity	1971	1962	1958
E_{EE}	−.92	−1.12	−.97
E_{OO}	−2.82	−.77	−1.72
E_{GG}	−1.47	−1.91	−1.87
E_{CC}	−1.52	−1.71	−1.61
E_{EO}	.23	.08	.21
E_{EG}	.20	.46	.25
E_{EC}	.04	.10	.00
E_{OE}	.74	.18	.63
E_{OG}	1.03	.03	.37
E_{OC}	.63	.07	.20
E_{GE}	.35	.51	.75
E_{GO}	.44	.12	.34
E_{GC}	.25	.60	.26
E_{CE}	.07	.90	.09
E_{CO}	.69	.05	.34
E_{CG}	.28	.48	.67

Allowing aggregate energy to vary increases the absolute magnitudes of the own-price elasticities. Elasticities involving the price of electric energy are affected the most, since the price of electric energy has the greatest effect on the price of aggregate energy input. The estimate of the own-price elasticity for electric energy in 1971 becomes −0.92, which is comparable to the estimate of −1.24 obtained in Chapter 5 for aggregate manufacturing in 1969. The estimate of E_{EG}^{T} in chapter 5, 0.23, is very close to the estimate of 0.20 shown in Table 8-12 for 1971.

Tests of Hypotheses

As shown in Tables 8-7 through 8-9, the estimated elasticities of demand vary across years. Changes in estimated elasticities over time may be due simply to changes in the cost shares or may reflect changes in the estimated parameters of the unit cost function caused by technological change. To test for structural change in the technology, the data for 1971 and 1962 are pooled and F tests are performed for constancy over time of the estimated parameters.[17] The test statistic is

$$F(k, n - 2k) = \frac{[SSR_p - (SSR_{62} + SSR_{71})]/k}{(SSR_{62} + SSR_{71})/k(n - 2)}$$

where SSR_p = residual sum of squares of the joint regression

        SSR_{62} = residual sum of squares of the 1962 regression when run separately

        SSR_{71} = residual sum of squares of the 1971 regression when run separately

        n = total number of observations in the pooled data set

        k = number of parameters estimated

It is possible to compute the test statistic for 13 industries for which the model performed well in 1971 and 1962. Test results are shown in Table 8-13. The null hypothesis of no change in the estimated parameters between the two years is rejected at the 1 percent level for 8 of the industries. Thus at least some of the differences in the estimated elasticities of demand apparently reflect changes over time in the parameters of the cost function as a result of technological change.

The translog form used here is less restrictive than the Cobb-Douglas form used in many earlier studies of production. If the energy-input function were Cobb-Douglas, all cross-elasticities of substitution would be equal to unity. The magnitudes of the estimated elasticities of substitution in Table 8-10 appear to

Table 8-13
Tests for Structural Change in Technology: Manufacturing

Industry	Degrees of Freedom	Test Statistic	Critical Value[a]
20	9, 158	5.94[b]	2.41
23	5, 59	0.76	3.34
24	5, 74	1.71	3.30
26	9, 126	4.94[b]	2.56
27	5, 59	1.22	3.34
28	9, 150	3.43[b]	2.41
29	5, 68	3.11	3.32
30	9, 98	5.56[b]	2.62
32	9, 122	4.64[b]	2.56
33	9, 98	3.05[b]	2.62
34	5, 116	14.26[b]	3.18
35	9, 70	0.38	2.70
36	5, 107	4.16[b]	3.22

[a]Significance level is .01.
[b]The null hypothesis of no structural change is rejected.

indicate that the energy-input function is not Cobb-Douglas, but it is preferable to test this hypothesis statistically. Since the Cobb-Douglas form is a special case of the translog form, it is possible to perform statistical tests for each industry of whether the more restrictive form is appropriate for the unit cost function. The tests will be equivalent to tests of whether the input function is Cobb-Douglas, because the Cobb-Douglas form is self-dual.

The restrictions on the translog form that cause it to collapse to the Cobb-Douglas form are

$$\gamma_{ij} = 0 \quad i, j = E, O, G, C$$

These restrictions are tested using the log-likelihood function. Test results are shown in Table 8–14. The null hypothesis that the unit cost function is Cobb-Douglas is rejected at the 5 percent level for 6 of 10 industries in 1971, 6 of 11 in 1962, and 9 of 10 in 1958.

Concluding Comments

Estimation of systems of demand equations derived from translog unit cost functions provides estimates of elasticities of demand and substitution that are

Table 8–14
Tests of Cobb-Douglas Functional Form: Manufacturing

	1971		1962		1958	
Industry	Test Statistic	Critical Value[a]	Test Statistic	Critical Value[a]	Test Statistic	Critical Value[a]
20	N/E		N/E		25.7[b]	12.6
22	N/E		11.2	12.6	N/E	
23	4.8	7.8	2.3	7.8	N/E	
24	N/E		10.6[b]	7.8	8.9[b]	7.8
25	N/E		8.4	12.6	N/E	
26	16.6[b]	12.6	21.8[b]	12.6	17.5[b]	12.6
27	N/E		3.4	7.8	N/E	
28	19.2[b]	12.6	N/E		25.4[b]	7.8
29	4.1	7.8	14.6[b]	7.8	N/E	
30	14.4[b]	12.6	N/E		N/E	
32	13.9[b]	12.6	13.0[b]	12.6	12.8[b]	12.6
33	15.2[b]	12.6	23.3[b]	12.6	17.0[b]	7.8
34	4.3	12.6	N/E		4.3	12.6
35	21.9[b]	12.6	5.3	12.6	21.7[b]	12.6
36	4.9	7.8	40.6[b]	12.6	14.8[b]	7.8
37	N/E		N/E		12.2[b]	7.8

[a]Significance level is .05.
[b]The null hypothesis that the form is Cobb-Douglas is rejected.
N/E means not estimated.

subject to only those restrictions implied by economic theory. Disaggregation of the analysis to the two-digit industry level allows for variation across industries in the characteristics of demand for each type of energy.

The model performs well for industries accounting for most of the consumption of energy in manufacturing in each year. The results indicate considerable variation in energy substitution both across industries and across types of energy. Aggregate manufacturing demand for energy appears to be highly price responsive. Estimated own-price elasticities for all types of energy except electric energy are generally substantially greater than unity.

Two points should be noted with respect to the interpretation of the estimated elasticities for analysis of public policies toward energy. First, since cross-section data are used, the estimates presumably reflect the long-run effects of prices on energy demand. Short-run effects can be expected to be considerably smaller. Second, the elasticities do not measure the net effects of price changes on consumption of fuel oil, gas, and coal. Because these fuels are inputs in the production of electricity, the net effects of price changes for these fuels will include changes in the demand for fuels in electric power generation. As discussed in the preceeding chapter, demand for fuels for electric power generation appears to be significantly responsive to fuel prices.

Notes

1. Electricity demand studies include Fisher and Kayser (1962) and Mount, Chapman, and Tyrell (1973).

2. Berndt and Wood (1975) and Griffen and Gregory (1976) consider the demand for aggregate energy and other inputs in aggregate manufacturing. Berndt and Jorgenson (1973) and Fuss (1977) consider the demand for individual types of energy by total U.S. and total Canadian manufacturing respectively.

3. Because the equations are estimated with an iterative Zellner-efficient procedure, the estimates of the parameters are invariant to the system of cost-share equations estimated.

4. Consumption of residual and distillate oil is reported separately. The quantity of fuel oil is computed by weighting the number of barrels of each type of oil by kilowatt-hours using conversion factors published in the *Census of Manufactures*. The use of prices as weights provided very similar results.

5. Thus the price data are equal to average prices. As discussed in Chapter 2, the use of declining rate schedules for electricity and gas results in a divergence between marginal and average prices for these inputs. Average prices are used because aggregate data on marginal prices are not available.

6. Use of a .01 significance level would result in rejection of the cross-equation equality restrictions for an additional four industries in 1971 and five in 1962 and 1958.

7. The monotonicity test at the means of the data can be interpreted as a local test at the point of expansion, see Jorgenson and Lau (1975).

8. Note that the concavity condition appears to be violated for three of the six observations for which the cross-equation equality restrictions are rejected.

9. Results for 1971 for the industries for which the model did not perform well are given in Tables 8A-1 and 8A-2.

10. Results shown are for the initial regressions; there was no sequential estimation.

11. Not having the elasticities of demand constrained to be constant is one of the major advantages of the use of a flexible functional form for the unit cost function.

12. The total number of estimated elasticities for each year is equal to the sum over industries of the number of own- and cross-elasticities for each industry times the number of observations for that industry. For 1971 the total number of estimated elasticities is 3378.

13. The cross-price elasticities should generally be smaller because the sum of the own- and cross-price elasticities is zero and most of the cross-price elasticities are positive.

14. An additional 15 of the positive estimates are significant at the 10 percent level in 1971.

15. For elasticities involving coal, the weights are the shares of each industry in total purchases by the industries for which the four-input model performed well.

16. Since the estimates of E_{HV} are obtained holding manufacturing output constant, these elasticities do not reflect induced output effects on energy demand.

17. Data for 1958 are not included in the pooled regressions because 1958 was a recession year and therefore not fully comparable with 1971 and 1962.

**Appendix 8A
Results for Other
Industries, 1971**

Table 8A-1
Parameter Estimates: Other Industries, 1971[a]

Parameter	Industry								
	20	22	24	25	27	31	37	38	39
α_E	.521[b] (.014)	.653[b] (.020)	.716[b] (.022)	.764[b] (.030)	.802[b] (.015)	.805[b] (.040)	.657[b] (.006)	.704[b] (.022)	.665[b] (.028)
α_O	.127[b] (.017)	.202[b] (.022)	.119[b] (.015)	.079[b] (.013)	.067[b] (.010)	.111[b] (.023)	.085[b] (.018)	.139[b] (.019)	.156[b] (.017)
α_G	.276[b] (.018)	.145[b] (.010)	.165[b] (.026)	.157[b] (.019)	.131[b] (.012)	.084[b] (.035)	.166[b] (.012)	.157[b] (.013)	.179[b] (.020)
α_C	.077[b] (.012)	N/E	N/E	N/E	N/E	N/E	.092[b] (.009)	N/E	N/E
γ_{EE}	.208[b] (.088)	-.043 (.074)	.196[b] (.088)	-.288 (.165)	.151 (.085)	.106[b] (.037)	-.057 (.053)	.260[b] (.107)	.163 (.197)
γ_{EO}	-.123 (.065)	.153[b] (.057)	-.088[b] (.045)	-.079 (.070)	-.083 (.046)	-.055[b] (.023)	.108 (.088)	-.019 (.068)	-.138 (.134)
γ_{EG}	-.223[b] (.066)	-.110[b] (.046)	-.107 (.083)	.367[b] (.108)	-.067 (.056)	-.051 (.032)	-.114 (.072)	-.241[b] (.073)	-.030 (.102)
γ_{EC}	.138[b] (.042)	N/E	N/E	N/E	N/E	N/E	.064[b] (.029)	N/E	N/E
γ_{OO}	-.043 (.067)	-.309[b] (.062)	-.058 (.041)	.109[b] (.037)	.014 (.038)	-.075 (.050)	-.630[b] (.256)	-.132[b] (.061)	-.059 (.112)
γ_{OG}	.209[b] (.058)	.156[b] (.028)	.146[b] (.048)	-.030 (.046)	.069[b] (.029)	.130[b] (.043)	.612[b] (.198)	.151[b] (.041)	.198[b] (.057)
γ_{OC}	-.043 (.037)	N/E	N/E	N/E	N/E	N/E	-.089 (.077)	N/E	N/E
γ_{GG}	.059 (.079)	-.046 (.042)	-.039 (.100)	-.338[b] (.082)	-.002 (.046)	-.079 (.047)	-.485[b] (.176)	.090 (.069)	-.168[b] (.075)

γ_{GC}	−.044 (.045)	N/E	N/E	N/E	N/E	N/E	−.012 (.059)	N/E	N/E
γ_{CC}	−.050 (.038)	N/E	N/E	N/E	N/E	N/E	.037 (.046)	N/E	N/E
Number of Observations	24	16	17	9	14	6	9	9	15

[a]Figures in parentheses are asymptotic standard errors.
[b]Significant at the .05 level.
N/E means not estimated.

Table 8A-2
Estimates of Price Elasticities: Other Industries, 1971[a]

Elasticity	Industry								
	20	22	24	25	27	31	37	38	39
E_{EE}	-.079 (.169)	-.413[b] (.114)	-.011 (.124)	-.613[b] (.253)	-.011 (.106)	-.063 (.069)	-.430[b] (.081)	.074 (.153)	-.082 (.294)
E_{OO}	-1.211[b] (.523)	-2.328[b] (.355)	-1.370[b] (.348)	.458 (.588)	-.725 (.508)	-1.568[b] (.418)	-8.336[b] (3.407)	-1.806[b] (.467)	-1.224[b] (.718)
E_{GG}	-.511[b] (.288)	-1.172[b] (.293)	-1.072[b] (.613)	-2.994[b] (.718)	-.882[b] (.352)	-1.848[b] (.638)	-3.753[b] (1.079)	-.268 (.440)	-1.759[b] (.457)
E_{CC}	-1.574[b] (.518)	N/E	N/E	N/E	N/E	N/E	-.504 (.499)	N/E	N/E
E_{EO}	-.109 (.125)	.437[b] (.092)	-.005 (.065)	-.025 (.107)	-.036 (.058)	.042 (.041)	.249 (.135)	.112 (.098)	-.052 (.200)
E_{EG}	-.152 (.126)	-.024 (.071)	.015 (.118)	.638[b] (.166)	.047 (.069)	.021 (.063)	-.008 (.110)	-.185 (.104)	.134 (.152)
E_{EC}	.341[b] (.080)	N/E	N/E	N/E	N/E	N/E	.189[b] (.045)	N/E	N/E
E_{OE}	-.450 (.526)	1.410[b] (.297)	-.029 (.344)	-.240 (1.040)	-.430 (.690)	.308 (.261)	1.923 (1.073)	.566 (.492)	-.220 (.854)
E_{OG}	1.925[b] (.513)	.918[b] (.164)	1.398[b] (.437)	-.218 (.693)	1.155[b] (.428)	1.259[b] (.425)	7.365[b] (2.803)	1.240[b] (.323)	1.444[b] (.372)
E_{OC}	-.264 (.295)	N/E	N/E	N/E	N/E	N/E	-.952 (.944)	N/E	N/E
E_{GE}	-.289 (.240)	-.108 (.322)	.066 (.510)	3.103[b] (.910)	.286 (.423)	.197 (.530)	-.032 (.436)	.831 (.475)	.497 (.572)
E_{GO}	.884[b] (.223)	1.281[b] (.215)	1.005[b] (.334)	-.109 (.347)	.596[b] (.219)	1.651 (.894)	3.768[b] (1.226)	1.099[b] (.267)	1.261[b] (.342)

E_{GC}	−.085 (.165)	N/E	N/E	N/E	N/E	N/E	.016 (.355)	N/E	N/E
E_{CE}	2.314[b] (.626)	N/E	N/E	N/E	N/E	N/E	1.356[b] (.326)	N/E	N/E
E_{CO}	−.436 (.479)	N/E	N/E	N/E	N/E	N/E	−.882 (.848)	N/E	N/E
E_{CG}	−.304 (.593)	N/E	N/E	N/E	N/E	N/E	.030 (.644)	N/E	N/E

[a]Figures in parentheses are asymptotic standard errors.
[b]Significant at the .05 level.
N/E means not estimated.

Part III
Dynamic Models of Energy

9

Short-Run Elasticities of Demand for Residential Electricity

Introduction

The elasticities of demand for residential electricity estimated from cross-section data in Chapters 3 and 4 reflect the long-run responses of demand. Estimates of short-run elasticities of demand are also of interest because of their potential usefulness in short-run demand forecasting. In addition, estimates of short-run elasticities can be used to assess the effectiveness of using price to ration electricity during periods of temporary capacity shortages.[1] In this chapter, short-run residential electricity demand elasticities are estimated using alternative dynamic formulations of the demand equation. The elasticities are estimated with time-series data for individual states for the period 1961–1975.

The estimated short-run price elasticities are negative, as expected, and indicate that price is a significant determinant of demand in the short run. The estimated short-run income elasticities of demand indicate that changes in income may have either a positive or negative effect on demand in the short run. Estimates of national short-run elasticities are computed as weighted averages of the results for individual states. For the model that performed best, the estimated national short-run price and income elasticities are −0.58 and −0.18 respectively.

The Model

The use of average price data to estimate structural demand and price equations is not as well suited for time-series analysis as for cross-section analysis. In particular, the estimation of a reliable structural price equation is difficult because the regulatory process introduces lags of arbitrary length in the reaction of price to changes in the cost variables. However, the difficulties involved in estimating a reduced-form equation using typical electric bill (TEB) data are less for time-series analysis than for cross-section analysis. Measurement error resulting from the use of fixed weights in constructing the TEB data should be less for time-series data, and variation in a TEB variable over time is less likely to confound shifts in the price schedule with changes in its structure. Therefore, the procedure used in estimating short-run elasticities is to estimate reduced-form equations incorporating a TEB variable.

135

The structural price equation used in the derivation of the reduced form is assumed to be log-linear:

$$\ln P_t = d_t - f \ln Q_t + u_t \qquad (9.1)$$

where the subscript t indicates time, P is electricity price, Q is average quantity purchased per customer, and u is a disturbance term. The price of electricity varies over time as a result of both endogenous changes in quantity purchased and exogenous changes in cost. Exogenous changes in costs are assumed to affect only the intercept term of the price equation.

The magnitudes of the exogenous shifts in the price equation are measured with a TEB variable, B, which is an index of the total cost of a given quantity of electricity. For example, the TEB for 250 kWh is

$$B_t = \int_{q=0}^{q=250} d_t Q_t^{-f} dq$$

Integrating and taking logs,

$$\ln B_t = d_t + \ln k$$

where k is a constant. Solving for d_t and substituting in equation (9.1) yields the price equation:

$$\ln P_t = -\ln k + \ln B_t - f \ln Q_t + u_t \qquad (9.2)$$

The number of explanatory variables that can be included in the structural demand equation is limited by the relatively short length of the available time series. The final form of the demand equation estimated in Chapter 3 includes electricity price, income, gas price, heating degree days, average July temperature, percent rural population, average size of households, and time. However, not all these variables need to be included in the short-run equation.

Changes over time in the percentage of population living in rural areas, the average size of households, and, by definition, the time variable are in the form of steady trends. The dynamic formulations used for the estimated short-run equations make it unnecessary to explicitly include such time-trend variables in the equation. Heating degree days and average July temperature fluctuate from year to year, but omission of these variables will not cause serious specification errors because they are not significantly correlated with other variables.

The elasticity of demand with respect to gas price is only 0.04 for the long-run demand equation. In the short run, the effect of gas price on demand should be even smaller because it depends in general on the substitution of one type of appliance for another. As a result, omitting gas price from the short-run equation should not result in large specification biases. Since omitting gas price results in a large reduction in the degree of multicollinearity of the variables, it was decided to omit the gas price variable from the short-run equation.

Thus the only explanatory variables retained in the demand equation are electricity price and average per capita income. Allowing for lags in the response of demand to changes in price and income, and assuming a log-linear functional form, the demand equation can be written

$$\ln Q_t = a + \sum_{j=0}^{m} b_j \ln P_{t-j} + \sum_{k=0}^{n} c_k \ln Y_{t-k} + u_t \qquad (9.3)$$

In principle, the number of lagged values of P and Y to include in the equation could be determined by successively adding lagged values of the variables until the coefficients of all additional lagged values were insignificant. In practice this approach is not feasible because the lagged values of the variables are highly multicollinear. Therefore, it is necessary to place a priori restrictions on the lag structures.

A common set of restrictions is that the coefficients of lagged values of the variables decline geometrically, i.e.,

$$b_j = b(1 - \lambda_1)\lambda_1^j \qquad 0 \leqslant \lambda_1 < 1; j = 0, 1, \ldots, \infty \qquad (9.4)$$

$$c_k = c(1 - \lambda_2)\lambda_2^k \qquad 0 \leqslant \lambda_2 < 1; k = 0, 1, \ldots, \infty \qquad (9.5)$$

If it is further assumed that $\lambda_1 = \lambda_2 = \lambda$, then substitution from equations (9.4) and (9.5) into equation (9.3) and application of the Koyck transformation (1954) yields the demand equation:

$$\ln Q_t = a(1 - \lambda) + \lambda \ln Q_{t-1} + b(1 - \lambda) \ln P_t + c(1 - \lambda) \ln Y_t$$

$$+ u_t - \lambda u_{t-1} \qquad (9.6)$$

The assumption that the coefficients decline geometrically can be relaxed by allowing the coefficients of the current values of price and income to take any value, imposing the geometrically declining lag structure only after the current period,

$$b_j = b_j \qquad j = 0$$

$$b_j = b(1 - \lambda)\lambda^j \qquad j = 1, \ldots, \infty \qquad (9.7)$$

$$c_k = c_k \qquad k = 0$$

$$c_k = c(1 - \lambda)\lambda^k \qquad k = 1, \ldots, \infty \qquad (9.8)$$

Substitution from equations (9.7) and (9.8) into equation (9.3) and application of the Koyck transformation yields the demand equation:

$$\ln Q_t = a(1 - \lambda) + \lambda \ln Q_{t-1} + b_0 \ln P_t + [b - \lambda(b_0 + b)] \ln P_{t-1}$$

$$+ c_0 \ln Y_t + [c - \lambda(c_0 + c)] \ln Y_{t-1} + u_t - \lambda u_{t-1} \quad (9.9)$$

An alternative approach is to derive the dynamic structure of the demand equations from explicit behavioral assumptions. Well-known examples of such models are the partial-adjustment and adaptive-expectations models, both of which yield demand equations of the same form as equation (9.6) (Johnston 1972, pp. 298–302). The dynamic structure can also be derived from consideration of the possible effects of habit formation on a consumer's behavior, as discussed below.

The influence of habitual levels of consumption can be incorporated in the demand equation by the inclusion of a variable for the "psychological stock" of habits at the beginning of the period:

$$\ln Q_t = a + b \ln P_t + c \ln Y_t + d \ln S_t + u_t \quad (9.10)$$

where S_t is the stock of habits at the beginning of period t. Because S_t is not observable, it is necessary to postulate a relationship between the stock of habits and observable variables.

One plausible behavioral assumption is that the stock of habits is a function of all past consumption levels, with the influence of successive lagged values decreasing geometrically. In log-linear form,

$$\ln S_t = e + f(1 - \lambda) \sum_{j=1}^{\infty} \lambda^{j-1} \ln Q_{t-j} \quad 0 \leqslant \lambda < 1 \quad (9.11)$$

Substituting in equation (9.10) from equation (9.11) and applying the Koyck transformation yields the demand equation:

$$\ln Q_t = (1 - \lambda)(a + de) + [df(1 - \lambda) + \lambda] \ln Q_{t-1}$$

$$+ b \ln P_t - b\lambda \ln P_{t-1} + c \ln Y_t - c\lambda \ln Y_{t-1} + u_t - \lambda u_{t-1} \quad (9.12)$$

which has the same form as equation (9.9).

Other assumptions with regard to the habit-formation process also result in demand equations of the same form as equation (9.9). For example, it might be assumed that[2]

$$\ln S_t = e + f \ln Q_{t-1} + g \ln S_{t-1} \quad 0 \leqslant g < 1 \quad (9.13)$$

By successive substitution, equation (9.13) can be written

$$\ln S_t = \frac{e}{1 - g} + f \sum_{j=1}^{\infty} g^{j-1} \ln Q_{t-j} \qquad (9.14)$$

Substituting in equation (9.10) from equation (9.14) and applying the Koyck transformation yields the demand equation:

$$\ln Q_t = (1 - g)a + de + (df + g)\ln Q_{t-1} + b \ln P_t$$
$$+ bg \ln P_{t-1} + c \ln Y_t - cg \ln Y_{t-1} + u_t - gu_{t-1} \quad (9.15)$$

In summary, dynamic demand equations have been derived for a number of assumptions. The equation

$$\ln Q_t = A_0 + A_1 \ln Q_{t-1} + A_2 \ln P_t + A_3 \ln Y_t + v_t \qquad (9.16)$$

is the general form of the demand equation derived from an equation incorporating geometrically declining coefficients, from the partial-adjustment model, and from the adaptive-expectations model. In each case, the short-run price and income elasticities are equal to A_2 and A_3 respectively. The long-run price elasticity is equal to $A_2/(1 - A_1)$, and the long-run income elasticity is equal to $A_3/(1 - A_1)$.

The equation

$$\ln Q_t = A_0 + A_1 \ln Q_{t-1} + A_2 \ln P_t + A_3 \ln P_{t-1} + A_4 \ln Y_t$$
$$+ A_5 \ln Y_{t-1} + v_t \quad (9.17)$$

is the general form of the demand equation derived from an equation in which the coefficients of the current values of price and income are left free but the coefficients of all lagged values of these variables are assumed to decline geometrically. It is also the general form of the demand equations derived from habit-formation models. Short-run price and income elasticities are equal to A_2 and A_4 respectively. The long-run price and income elasticities are equal to $A_3/(1 - A_1)$ and $A_5(1 - A_1)$ respectively.

Estimation Procedures

Because it is not possible to choose among the alternative formulations on a priori grounds, reduced-form equations are estimated for models containing both the dynamic demand equations, (9.16) and (9.17). The reduced-form equation for quantity purchased is obtained for each model by substituting for price in the demand equation using equation (9.2), which can be rewritten

$$\ln P_t = C_0 + C_1 \ln Q_t + \ln B_t + u_t \qquad (9.18)$$

For example, the reduced-form equation for quantity purchased for a model incorporating equation (9.16) is

$$\ln Q_t = \frac{A_0 + A_2 C_0}{1 - A_2 C_1} + \frac{A_1}{1 - A_2 C_1} \ln Q_{t-1} + \frac{A_2}{1 - A_2 C_1} \ln B_t$$
$$+ \frac{A_3}{1 - A_2 C_1} \ln Y_t + w_t \qquad (9.19)$$

The coefficient of B_t in (9.19) is equal to the total short-run elasticity of demand with respect to a shift in the price schedule, and the coefficient of Y_t is equal to the total short-run elasticity of demand with respect to income. Long-run elasticities of demand cannot be derived from the coefficients of equation (9.19).

The variables in equation (9.19) can be assumed to be independent of the contemporaneous disturbance term. Therefore, estimation inconsistency resulting from the dependence of price on quantity purchased is eliminated. However, the inclusion of lagged dependent variables on the righthand side of the reduced-form equation will cause ordinary least squares (OLS) estimates to be inconsistent if the disturbance term is serially correlated. In order to test for first-order serial correlation, the reduced-form equations are estimated by both OLS and a Cochrane-Orcutt procedure (Cochrane and Orcutt 1949).

The OLS and Cochrane-Orcutt (CO) results are compared using the F-statistic:

$$F(1, n - k - 1) = \frac{SSR_{OLS} - SSR_{CO}}{SSR_{CO}/n - k - 1} \qquad (9.20)$$

where n is the number of observations, k is the number of parameters estimated, SSR is the sum of squared residuals, and the subscripts indicate the estimation procedure. This test is equivalent to a test of the null hypothesis that the first-order serial correlation coefficient is equal to zero.

The equations are estimated with annual data for the 48 contiguous states[3] for the period 1961–1975.[4] Average sales per customer are calculated from data on total residential sales and average number of residential customers in Edison Electric Institute (various). Typical electric bill (TEB) data are for a consumption level of 250 kilowatt-hours per month and are from the Federal Power Commission (various). Data on average income per capita are from U.S. Department of Commerce (various). The price and income variables are expressed in real terms by deflating them by the consumer price index.

Elasticity Estimates

Estimates of the short-run elasticities of demand obtained for the model incorporating equation (9.16) are shown in Table 9-1, and estimates for the model incorporating (9.17) are shown in Table 9-2. The results obtained with OLS are presented if the null hypothesis of no first-order serial correlation is not rejected at the 10 percent level, and the Cochrane-Orcutt results are presented otherwise. The null hypothesis is rejected for 32 states for the model incorporating equation (9.16) and for 8 states for the model incorporating equation (9.17). The estimation procedure used for each state is noted in the tables.

The estimated own-price elasticities are negative for all but one state for the model incorporating equation (9.16). Moreover, 40 of the 47 negative estimates are significant at the 5 percent level using one-tailed t-tests. The one positive estimate is not significant. All estimated price elasticities are negative for the model incorporating equation (9.17), but only 25 are significant at the 5 percent level. In addition to a lower level of significance, the estimated price elasticities obtained using equation (9.17) tend to be smaller in absolute magnitude. The mean of the estimates is -0.78 using (9.16) and -0.48 using (9.17).

The results with respect to the estimated income elasticities are quite surprising. Only 25 of the estimates are positive for the model incorporating equation (9.16), of which 23 are significant at the 5 percent level using two-tailed t tests. The remaining 23 estimated income elasticities are negative, of which 11 are significant. The frequency of negative estimates is even more marked for the model incorporating equation (9.17). Only 15 of the estimates are positive, and only one of these is significant at the 5 percent level. Of the 33 negative estimates, 15 are significant.

Since the income elasticity of demand for electricity is usually assumed to be positive, it is desirable to check whether the negative estimates obtained here are the result of misspecification of the models. The most plausible source of specification error common to both models is the assumption that price and income have the same lag coefficients. The effects of this assumption can be tested by estimating models in which the lag coefficients of price and income are not constrained to be equal.

If it is assumed that the lag coefficients satisfy equations (9.4) and (9.5), with $\lambda_1 \neq \lambda_2$, the demand equation becomes

$$\ln Q_t = a(1 - \lambda_1)(1 - \lambda_2) + (\lambda_1 + \lambda_2) \ln Q_{t-1} - \lambda_1\lambda_2 \ln Q_{t-2}$$
$$+ b(1 - \lambda_1) \ln P_t - b(1 - \lambda_1)\lambda_2 \ln P_{t-1} + c(1 - \lambda_2) \ln Y_t$$
$$- c(1 - \lambda_2)\lambda_1 \ln Y_{t-1} + u_t - (\lambda_1 + \lambda_2)u_{t-1} + \lambda_1\lambda_2 u_{t-2} \quad (9.21)$$

Of the 48 estimated short-run income elasticities obtained for the model incorporating equation (9.21), 21 are positive and 27 are negative. Thus the existence of negative estimates cannot be attributed to the assumption of equal lag coefficients for price and income.

While the frequency of negative estimates of the short-run income elasticities could be the result of some other specification error, it appears more likely that the short-run income elasticities are in fact negative in a number of states. The existence of negative short-run income elasticities need not be inconsistent with the assumption that electricity is a normal good in the long run. Variations in electricity consumption in the short run will mainly involve changes in the utilization rate of existing electric equipment. If the short-run income elasticity of activity outside the home is greater than that of activity within the home, changes in income will be negatively related to the utilization rate of existing equipment, resulting in negative short-run income elasticities of demand for electricity.

Tests of Dynamic Specification

As shown in Tables 9-1 and 9-2, estimates of short-run price and income elasticities obtained with the models incorporating equations (9.16) and (9.17) are quite dissimilar in magnitude for most states. Therefore, it is important to consider which of the models is correct. It is not possible to choose between the models on a priori grounds, but a statistical test of which model performs best is available.

Equation (9.16) can be treated as a special case of equation (9.17) in which the coefficients of P_{t-1} and Y_{t-1} have been constrained to equal zero. Therefore, the two specifications can be compared by testing the null hypothesis that the coefficients of P_{t-1} and Y_{t-1} are equal to zero in equation (9.17). The test statistic is

$$F(2, k) = \frac{(SSR_U - SRR_R)/2}{SSR_U/k}$$

where SSR is the sum of squared residuals, the subscripts U and R refer to the models incorporating equations (9.17) and (9.16) respectively, and k is the number of degrees of freedom for the model. The value of k is eight for equations estimated by OLS and seven for equations estimated with the Cochrane-Orcutt (CO) procedure.

As shown in Tables 9-1 and 9-2, the CO procedure generally performed better for the model incorporating equation (9.16), and OLS generally per-

Table 9–1
Estimates of Short-Run Elasticities:
Model Incorporating Equation 9.16[a]

State	Own-Price Elasticity	Income Elasticity	R^2	Estimation Procedure[b]
Maine	−0.298[c] (0.069)	0.132[c] (0.071)	.9972	CO
New Hampshire	−0.322[c] (0.093)	−0.462[c] (0.082)	.9888	CO
Vermont	−0.575[c] (0.101)	−0.212[c] (0.088)	.9815	CO
Massachusetts	−0.809[c] (0.130)	−0.033 (0.112)	.9879	CO
Rhode Island	−0.691[c] (0.141)	−0.147 (0.122)	.9855	CO
Connecticut	−0.434[c] (0.141)	−0.316[c] (0.119)	.9721	CO
New York	−0.639[c] (0.124)	−0.182 (0.104)	.9799	CO
New Jersey	−0.644[c] (0.124)	−0.176 (0.104)	.9814	CO
Pennsylvania	−0.428[c] (0.119)	−0.346[c] (0.101)	.9835	CO
Ohio	−1.142[c] (0.218)	0.928[c] (0.169)	.9189	CO
Indiana	−0.702[c] (0.163)	0.455[c] (0.077)	.9962	CO
Illinois	−1.595[c] (0.080)	0.640[c] (0.066)	.9992	OLS
Michigan	−1.151[c] (0.066)	0.280[c] (0.055)	.9993	OLS
Wisconsin	0.112 (0.164)	−0.793[c] (0.140)	.9919	CO
Minnesota	−1.213[c] (0.055)	0.356[c] (0.046)	.9995	OLS
Iowa	−1.254[c] (0.041)	0.398[c] (0.035)	.9997	OLS
Missouri	−1.610[c] (0.100)	0.669[c] (0.084)	.9987	OLS
North Dakota	−0.991[c] (0.034)	0.198[c] (0.030)	.9996	OLS
South Dakota	−1.168[c] (0.075)	0.372[c] (0.086)	.9882	CO
Nebraska	−1.400[c] (0.177)	0.552[c] (0.186)	.9476	CO
Kansas	−1.136[c] (0.281)	−0.226 (0.158)	.9860	CO

Table 9-1 Continued

State	Own-Price Elasticity	Income Elasticity	R^2	Estimation Procedure[b]
Delaware	−0.288[c] (0.141)	−0.437[c] (0.119)	.9775	CO
Maryland–D.C.	−0.376[c] (0.050)	1.128[c] (0.185)	.9962	CO
Virginia	−0.814[c] (0.234)	1.107[c] (0.121)	.9229	CO
West Virginia	−0.218[c] (0.116)	0.148 (0.168)	.9975	OLS
North Carolina	−0.290 (0.162)	−0.450[c] (0.144)	.9841	CO
South Carolina	−0.150 (0.214)	−0.592[c] (0.193)	.9811	CO
Georgia	−0.585[c] (0.231)	−0.210 (0.201)	.9884	CO
Florida	−1.308[c] (0.016)	0.482[c] (0.014)	.9877	CO
Kentucky	−1.468[c] (0.096)	0.553[c] (0.082)	.9975	OLS
Tennessee	−0.227 (0.215)	−0.430[c] (0.182)	.9431	CO
Alabama	−0.549[c] (0.270)	1.203[c] (0.102)	.9493	CO
Mississippi	−1.649[c] (0.072)	0.755[c] (0.063)	.9987	OLS
Arkansas	−0.025 (0.468)	−0.117 (0.346)	.9906	OLS
Louisiana	−1.265[c] (0.185)	0.394[c] (0.172)	.9917	CO
Oklahoma	−1.389[c] (0.046)	0.500[c] (0.040)	.9994	OLS
Texas	−1.024 (0.890)	0.196 (0.756)	.8285	OLS
Montana	−0.958[c] (0.070)	0.149[c] (0.060)	.9991	OLS
Idaho	−0.585[c] (0.128)	−0.130 (0.111)	.9839	CO
Wyoming	−0.728[c] (0.065)	−0.106 (0.064)	.9713	CO
Colorado	−0.795[c] (0.092)	−0.052 (0.090)	.9635	CO
New Mexico	−1.051[c] (0.035)	0.184[c] (0.031)	.9998	OLS
Arizona	−0.660[c] (0.336)	−0.123 (0.295)	.9732	CO

Table 9-1 Continued

State	Own-Price Elasticity	Income Elasticity	R^2	Estimation Procedure[b]
Utah	−1.073[c] (0.036)	0.211[c] (0.030)	.9998	OLS
Nevada	−0.908[c] (0.053)	0.162[c] (0.043)	.9994	OLS
Washington	−0.280 (0.158)	−0.369[c] (0.128)	.9799	CO
Oregon	−0.387[c] (0.173)	−0.269 (0.144)	.9695	CO
California	−0.297 (0.208)	−0.463[c] (0.172)	.9862	CO

[a]Figures in parentheses are estimated standard errors.
[b]OLS is ordinary least squares; CO is Cochrane-Orcutt.
[c]Significant at the .05 level.

Table 9-2
Estimates of Short-Run Elasticities:
Model Incorporating Equation 9.17[a]

State	Own-Price Elasticity	Income Elasticity	R^2	Estimation Procedure[b]
Maine	−0.240[c] (0.123)	−0.011 (0.234)	.9971	OLS
New Hampshire	−0.399[c] (0.073)	−0.376[c] (0.064)	.9998	OLS
Vermont	−0.211[c] (0.078)	−0.526[c] (0.068)	.9999	OLS
Massachusetts	−0.442[c] (0.138)	−0.345[c] (0.119)	.9999	OLS
Rhode Island	−0.050 (0.183)	−0.700[c] (0.158)	.9999	OLS
Connecticut	−0.069 (0.106)	0.254 (0.285)	.9950	CO
New York	−0.477[c] (0.117)	−0.320[c] (0.099)	.9935	CO
New Jersey	−0.461[c] (0.115)	−0.324[c] (0.096)	.9998	OLS
Pennsylvania	−0.220[c] (0.098)	−0.517[c] (0.083)	.9999	OLS
Ohio	−0.279[c] (0.103)	−0.456[c] (0.087)	.9999	OLS

Table 9–2 Continued

State	Own-Price Elasticity	Income Elasticity	R^2	Estimation Procedure[b]
Indiana	−0.285 (0.220)	0.137 (0.144)	.9981	OLS
Illinois	−0.144 (0.427)	−0.574 (0.357)	.9997	OLS
Michigan	−0.382[c] (0.163)	−0.370[c] (0.137)	.9876	OLS
Wisconsin	−0.062 (0.160)	−0.627[c] (0.134)	.9999	OLS
Minnesota	−0.428[c] (0.202)	−0.319 (0.174)	.9998	OLS
Iowa	−0.327 (0.348)	−0.406 (0.302)	.9998	OLS
Missouri	−0.026 (0.400)	−0.686 (0.342)	.9996	OLS
North Dakota	−0.681[c] (0.164)	−0.078 (0.146)	.9997	OLS
South Dakota	−0.801[c] (0.148)	0.018 (0.132)	.9998	OLS
Nebraska	−0.397[c] (0.193)	0.273 (0.187)	.9910	CO
Kansas	−0.383 (0.625)	0.008 (0.388)	.9845	OLS
Delaware	−0.397[c] (0.155)	−0.339[c] (0.134)	.9859	OLS
Maryland–D.C.	−0.110 (0.142)	0.490 (0.457)	.9970	OLS
Virginia	−0.828[c] (0.087)	0.028 (0.076)	.9966	CO
West Virginia	−0.222[c] (0.096)	−0.134 (0.176)	.9987	OLS
North Carolina	−0.397[c] (0.159)	−0.338[c] (0.138)	.9997	OLS
South Carolina	−0.626[c] (0.146)	−0.147 (0.130)	.9933	CO
Georgia	−0.582[c] (0.253)	−0.198 (0.216)	.9997	OLS
Florida	−0.925[c] (0.074)	0.147 (0.066)	.9972	CO
Kentucky	−0.366 (0.421)	−0.401 (0.365)	.9987	OLS
Tennessee	−0.347 (0.214)	−0.314 (0.178)	.9994	OLS
Alabama	−0.157 (0.180)	−0.548[c] (0.153)	.9996	OLS
Mississippi	−1.104[c] (0.415)	0.265 (0.707)	.9990	OLS

Table 9-2 Continued

State	Own-Price Elasticity	Income Elasticity	R^2	Estimation Procedure[b]
Arkansas	−0.830 (0.521)	−0.497 (0.374)	.9947	OLS
Louisiana	−1.575[c] (0.702)	0.678 (0.619)	.9997	OLS
Oklahoma	−0.836 (1.424)	0.012 (1.254)	.9995	OLS
Texas	−2.928 (9.468)	1.854 (8.211)	.8300	OLS
Montana	−0.084 (0.174)	0.160 (0.287)	.9804	CO
Idaho	−0.471[c] (0.203)	−0.222 (0.174)	.9998	OLS
Wyoming	−0.966[c] (0.313)	0.116 (0.265)	.9997	OLS
Colorado	−0.540 (0.365)	−0.254 (0.310)	.9996	OLS
New Mexico	−0.382 (0.210)	−0.400 (0.183)	.9999	OLS
Arizona	−0.473 (0.268)	−0.271 (0.232)	.9995	OLS
Utah	−0.616[c] (0.121)	−0.175 (0.102)	.9999	OLS
Nevada	−0.206 (0.359)	1.039[c] (0.296)	.9822	CO
Washington	−0.053 (0.254)	−0.534[c] (0.200)	.9997	OLS
Oregon	−0.081 (0.539)	−0.509 (0.438)	.9997	OLS
California	−0.339 (0.216)	−0.415[c] (0.177)	.9999	OLS

[a]Figures in parentheses are estimated standard errors.
[b]OLS is ordinary least squares, CO is Cochrane-Orcutt.
[c]Significant at the .05 level.

formed better for the model incorporating equation (9.17). Since the same procedure generally did not perform better for both models, the test statistic is computed for each state for both the OLS and CO procedures. Test results are shown in Table 9-3. The results obtained using the OLS and CO procedures agree for 33 states. The null hypothesis that equation (9.16) is the correct specification is rejected at the 10 percent level for 25 of these states and is accepted for 8. Of the 15 states for which the OLS and CO results do not agree, the null hypothesis is rejected for the OLS procedure but accepted for the CO procedure for 13 states and is accepted for OLS but rejected for CO for 2 states. Thus the test results indicate that the performance of the model incorporating equation (9.17) is superior, especially for equations estimated by OLS.[5]

Concluding Comments

The estimation of dynamic reduced-form equations using time-series data provides estimates of the short-run total elasticities of demand. The results provide a basis for short-run demand forecasts at the state level and suggest that price rationing can be effective in the short run in at least some states.

Estimated short-run price and income elasticities for individual states are the most relevant for most policy purposes, but estimates of national short-run elasticities are also of some interest. Although pooling of the data for all states has to be rejected because of the heterogeneity of the state results, estimates of the national elasticities can be obtained by constructing weighted averages of the state estimates. Weighting by total residential sales per state in 1975 yields estimated national short-run total price and income elasticities of −0.58 and −0.18, respectively, for the model incorporating equation (9.17).[6]

Table 9-3
Tests of the Dynamic Specification of the Demand Equation

| | Test Statistic for Model Estimated By | |
State	OLS[a]	Cochrane-Orcutt[b]
Maine	1.01	0.73
New Hampshire	185.32[c]	4.02[c]
Vermont	409.33[c]	10.73[c]
Massachusetts	172.21[c]	6.20[c]
Rhode Island	208.15[c]	8.09[c]
Connecticut	202.00[c]	15.81[c]
New York	286.79[c]	7.25[c]
New Jersey	230.41[c]	6.77[c]
Pennsylvania	488.93[c]	7.32[c]
Ohio	83.94[c]	50.17[c]
Indiana	12.98[c]	3.60[c]
Illinois	6.12[c]	6.52[c]
Michigan	7.92[c]	9.69[c]
Wisconsin	51.85[c]	1.26
Minnesota	8.06[c]	6.27[c]
Iowa	3.59[c]	4.79[c]
Missouri	8.07[c]	6.64[c]
North Dakota	1.88	1.62
South Dakota	3.51[c]	0.86
Nebraska	17.04[c]	16.85[c]
Kansas	0.73	0.02
Delaware	103.85[c]	2.08

Table 9–3 Continued

State	Test Statistic for Model Estimated By	
	OLS[a]	Cochrane-Orcutt[b]
Maryland–D.C.	12.23[c]	0.92
Virginia	107.29[c]	76.10[c]
West Virginia	3.75[c]	2.37
North Carolina	26.90[c]	1.62
South Carolina	49.42[c]	6.34[c]
Georgia	26.94[c]	2.66
Florida	14.53[c]	12.22[c]
Kentucky	3.75[c]	3.57[c]
Tennessee	26.74[c]	1.41
Alabama	70.88[c]	10.55[c]
Mississippi	0.91	0.86
Arkansas	3.03	3.27[c]
Louisiana	3.36[c]	0.46
Oklahoma	0.60	0.44
Texas	0.04	0.51
Montana	8.46[c]	12.14[c]
Idaho	4.34[c]	1.22
Wyoming	3.07	1.38
Colorado	1.88	0.76
New Mexico	5.99[c]	6.62[c]
Arizona	16.83[c]	4.14[c]
Utah	7.51[c]	6.32[c]
Nevada	0.20	5.60[c]
Washington	15.80[c]	0.93
Oregon	5.77[c]	1.56
California	60.22[c]	1.63

[a]Critical value at 10 percent level is 3.11.
[b]Critical value at 10 percent level is 3.26.
[c]The null hypothesis that equation (9.16) is correct is rejected.

Notes

1. An example of the type of short-run capacity shortage in which price rationing might be considered is a drought-induced decrease in capacity for a system with significant hydroelectric generating capacity.

2. Houthakker and Taylor (1966) formulate a model in continuous time in which the habit formation equation is

$$\dot{S}_t = Q_t - hS_t$$

where $\dot{S}_t$ is the time derivative of the stock of habits and h is a constant depreciation rate. The discrete time analog in log-linear form is

$$\ln S_t - \ln S_{t-1} = \ln Q_{t-1} - h \ln S_{t-1}$$

or

$$\ln S_t = \ln Q_{t-1} + (1 - h) \ln S_{t-1}$$

which is a special case of equation (9.13) with $e = 0$ and $f = 1$.

3. The data for Maryland include data for the District of Columbia.

4. Data for years prior to 1961 are not included because the classification of customers used in reporting data changed in 1960.

5. The performance of models incorporating equations (9.17) and (9.21) can be compared by testing the null hypothesis that the coefficient of Q_{t-2} in the model incorporating (9.21) is equal to zero. The null hypothesis, which is equivalent to a test that equation (9.17) is the correct specification, is accepted for all states using OLS and for all but three states using the Cochrane-Orcutt procedure.

6. The estimated elasticities for Texas are the largest in absolute magnitude of any state but are very small relative to their standard errors. Omitting the results for Texas from the computation of the weighted average elasticities provides estimates of the national price and income elasticities of −0.40 and −0.33 respectively.

10 A Dynamic Model of Aggregate Energy Demand in Manufacturing

Introduction

The dynamic characteristics of energy demand in U.S. manufacturing remain largely unexplored. With the exception of some simple dynamic models of electricity demand (Mount, Chapman, and Tyrell 1973; Chern 1976), previous studies of energy demand in manufacturing have been based on static models. When applied to cross-section data, as in Chapter 8, static models can be interpreted as providing estimates of long-run elasticities of demand and substitution.[1] However, previous studies have generally used time-series data (Berndt and Jorgenson 1973; Berndt and Wood 1975; and Hudson and Jorgenson 1974). The use of static models in time-series analyses is appropriate only if all adjustments in quantities of inputs can be made instantaneously. If this condition is not satisfied, the estimation results will not provide unbiased estimates of either short-run or long-run elasticities.

In this chapter, the model of demand for factors of production developed by Nadiri and Rosen (1969, 1973) is adapted to estimate dynamic demand equations for energy and other inputs. The results include estimates of short-run, long-run, and intermediate-run price elasticities of demand. The results also include estimates of the response of demand for each input to temporary excess demands for other inputs. Pairs of inputs are defined as dynamic substitutes, if the response of each to excess demand for the other is positive, and dynamic complements, if the response is negative.

All estimated short-run elasticities of demand for energy are statistically significant. The responses to price changes are found to be quite rapid, with the full long-run responses being approximately realized within three years after the year in which a price change occurs.

The estimated long-run price elasticities indicate that capital and energy are complements and that labor and energy are substitutes in the long run. The estimated responses of demand to excess demands for other inputs indicate that capital and energy are also dynamic complements and that labor and energy are dynamic substitutes.

The Model

A twice-differentiable aggregate production function is assumed to exist for total U.S. manufacturing:

151

$$Y = Y(H, K, U, L, B, X)$$

where Y is total output, H is aggregate energy input, K is capital stock, U is the utilization rate of capital, L is labor stock, B is the utilization rate of labor, and X is a vector of all other inputs.

Stocks and utilization rates of capital and labor are entered separately since they are separate objects of choice by the firm. This specification differs from the usual procedure of combining stock and utilization rates into measures of input services.[2] The approach used here has the advantage of not constraining the dynamic responses of stock and utilization variables to be equal a priori.

Energy input is measured as a flow. The firm may hold stocks of some types of energy, but most energy is obtained directly from outside the firm. Therefore, it is not meaningful to break down energy input into stock and utilization rate components. The inputs in X could not be included explicitly in the model because adequate data are not available for them. The omission of these inputs from the empirical analysis will not bias the estimated elasticities if the production function is weakly separable in the energy, capital, and labor variables.

Following the procedure described in Chapter 6, input demand equations could be derived from a translog unit cost function. However, the full system of equations could not be estimated because data are not available on the prices or cost shares of capital utilization and labor stock. Therefore, the more traditional, and less desirable, approach of deriving demand equations from a restrictive functional form of the production function is used.

The functional form chosen for the production function is the Cobb-Douglas:[3]

$$\ln Q_t = \alpha_0 + \alpha_H \ln H_t + \alpha_K \ln K_t + \alpha_U \ln U_t + \alpha_L \ln L_t + \alpha_B \ln B \quad (10.1)$$

The firm is assumed to minimize costs subject to an output constraint. The firm's costs are

$$C = P_H H + P_K K + P_B(LB) + P_L L \quad (10.2)$$

where P_H is the price of energy, P_K is the user cost of the capital stock, P_B is the hourly wage rate, and P_L is the user cost of the labor stock. The utilization rate of capital, U, does not appear explicitly in equation (10.2) but appears implicitly through the effect of U on the depreciation rate and hence on P_K, $P_U = P_K \cdot dP_K/dP_U$.

Solving the static cost-minimization problem yields the long-run equilibrium demand equations shown in Table 10-1. The long-run demand equations have several interesting characteristics. First, the level of output has no effect on utilization rates in the long-run. Second, long-run utilization rates are independent of all cross-price effects except with respect to the price of the correspond-

Table 10-1
Long-Run Equilibrium Demand Equations: Manufacturing

$$
\begin{bmatrix} \ln H \\ \ln K \\ \ln U \\ \ln L \\ \ln B \end{bmatrix}
=
\begin{bmatrix} k_H \\ k_K \\ k_U \\ k_L \\ k_B \end{bmatrix}
+
\begin{bmatrix} \frac{1}{\rho} \\ \frac{1}{\rho} \\ 0 \\ \frac{1}{\rho} \\ 0 \end{bmatrix} [\ln Q]
+
\begin{bmatrix}
\frac{\alpha_H}{\rho} - 1 & \frac{\alpha_K - \alpha_U}{\rho} & \frac{\alpha_U}{\rho} & \frac{\alpha_L - \alpha_B}{\rho} & \frac{\alpha_B}{\rho} \\
\frac{\alpha_H}{\rho} & \frac{\alpha_K - \alpha_U}{\rho} - 1 & \frac{\alpha_U}{\rho} & \frac{\alpha_L - \alpha_B}{\rho} & \frac{\alpha_B}{\rho} \\
0 & +1 & -1 & 0 & 0 \\
\frac{\alpha_H}{\rho} & \frac{\alpha_K - \alpha_U}{\rho} & \frac{\alpha_U}{\rho} & \frac{\alpha_L - \alpha_B}{\rho} - 1 & \frac{\alpha_B}{\rho} \\
0 & 0 & 0 & +1 & -1
\end{bmatrix}
\begin{bmatrix} \ln P_H \\ \ln P_K \\ \ln P_U \\ \ln P_L \\ \ln P_B \end{bmatrix}
$$

Note: $\rho = \alpha_H + \alpha_K + \alpha_L$

ing stock variable. Third, the prices of the utilization inputs, P_U and P_B, affect the demand for energy positively.

The long-run demand equations can be written in matrix notation as

$$X^* = k + CQ + DR \qquad (10.3)$$

where all variables are in logarithmic form, X^* is a vector of optimal input demands, k is a vector of intercept terms, C is a vector of scale effects, Q is output, D is a matrix of factor price effects, and R is a vector of factor prices. Since the demand equations are log-linear, the elements of matrix D are equal to long-run price elasticities.

The firm will not be in long-run equilibrium at every point in time because of costs in adjusting inputs to their desired levels. A log-linear adjustment function is assumed

$$\ln X_{it} - \ln X_{it\text{-}1} = \sum_j \gamma_{ij}(\ln X_{jt}^* - \ln X_{jt\text{-}1}) + \epsilon_{it} \qquad i, j = H, K, U, L, B$$

$$(10.4)$$

where X_{it} is the quantity of input X_i in period t, X_{jt}^* is the desired or target level of input j in period t and is defined by equation (10.3), the γ_{ij} are fixed adjustment coefficients, and the ϵ_{ij} are random variables with zero means and constant variances.[4] The specification of the adjustment function allows the adjustment of each input to be affected by the level of "excess demand" for all inputs.

Writing equation (10.4) in matrix notation,

$$X_t = \Gamma X_t^* + (I - \Gamma)X_{t\text{-}1} + \epsilon_t \qquad (10.5)$$

where all variables are in logarithmic form, X_t is a vector of input quantities in period t, Γ is a matrix of adjustment coefficients, X_t^* is a vector of desired input quantities in period t, I is an identity matrix, and ϵ_t is a vector of error terms. The equations to be estimated are derived by substituting for X_t^* in equation (10.5) from equation (10.3):

$$X_t = \Gamma k + \Gamma CQ + \Gamma DR + (I - \Gamma)X_{t\text{-}1} + \epsilon_t \qquad (10.6)$$

The diagonal elements of Γ are own-adjustment coefficients and should satisfy the restriction $0 \leqslant \gamma_{ii} \leqslant 1$ for all i. The more variable the factor, the closer to unity will be the own-adjustment coefficient. The off-diagonal elements, γ_{ij}, indicate the effect on input i of excess demand for input j. The γ_{ij} can be either positive or negative. Assuming that the firm remains on its production function at all times, not all elements in any row of Γ can be of the same sign. Inputs must react positively to excess demand for some inputs and negatively to excess demand for others.[5]

The cross-adjustment coefficients should be symmetric in signs. Pairs of inputs with identically signed cross-adjustment coefficients can be identified as dynamic substitutes or dynamic complements. If γ_{ij} is positive, excess demand for input j increases the short-run demand for input i. Pairs of inputs for which cross-adjustment coefficients are positive are defined to be *dynamic substitutes*. If the cross-adjustment coefficients are negative, the inputs are defined to be *dynamic complements*. Because of short-run adjustment costs, inputs may be dynamic complements (substitutes) even though they are substitutes (complements) in the long run.

Because the input demand equations are log-linear, the elements of the matrix product ΓD are equal to the short-run price elasticities of demand. From equation (10.3), the long-run price elasticities are equal to the elements of matrix D. Given estimates of $(1 - \Gamma)$ and ΓD, the estimated long-run price elasticities are computed from $[I - (I - \Gamma)]^{-1}\Gamma D$.

The estimated response path of input demand to prices can be computed from $\Gamma_k = (I - \Gamma)^k \Gamma D$ (Nadiri and Rosen 1973, p. 75). Computation of

$$\Gamma_0 + \Gamma_1 + \ldots + \Gamma_n \qquad n = 0, 1, \ldots$$

provides a matrix of estimated price elasticities showing the extent to which demand responds during a length of time $n + 1$ periods long. Thus in addition to short-run and long-run price elasticities, the results provide estimates of all intermediate-run elasticities.

Dynamic stability of the system of demand equations requires that $(I - \Gamma)^n$ approaches zero as n gets large. This can be checked by determining if the absolute values of the characteristic roots of $(I - \Gamma)$ are less than unity. However, this procedure does not provide a statistical test of stability because the sampling distributions of the characteristic roots are unknown.

Empirical Results

The equations are estimated with annual data for total manufacturing for 1947–1971. Data availability requires some modifications in the system of equations to be estimated. The prices of labor stock and of capital utilization are omitted because of lack of data. Because data on the utilization rate of capital are not available, the utilization rate of capacity is used as a proxy for this variable. The distinction is important, since the capacity utilization rate reflects the utilization of all inputs, not just capital. Capacity utilization data are from Wharton (1976).

The relevant output variable is the equilibrium level of output perceived by the firm. As measures of this variable, shipments and shipments plus changes in inventories are included in alternative specifications of the demand equations. Data on shipments and inventories are from U.S. Bureau of the Census (1976). The output variables are deflated by the wholesale price index for manufactured goods from U.S. Bureau of Labor Statistics (various).

Data on capital stock, rental price of capital, energy input, and energy price are from Berndt and Wood (1975). Data on labor stock and the utilization rate of labor are from U.S. Department of Labor (1976). The stock of labor is equal to the total number of employees in manufacturing. Average weekly hours of production workers is used as the labor utilization variable. Data on the price of labor utilization, defined as the quality-adjusted wage rate, are from Berndt and Wood (1975).

In order to impose homogeneity of degree zero in prices, the demand equations are expressed in terms of price ratios. The equations are then:

$$\ln X_{it} = a_i + b_i \ln Q_t + c_{1i} \ln (P_H/P_B) + c_{2i} \ln (P_K/P_B) + g_{1i} \ln H_{t-1}$$
$$+ g_{2i} \ln K_{t-1} + g_{3i} \ln U_{t-1} + g_{4i} \ln L_{t-1} + g_{5i} \ln B_{t-1} + \epsilon_{it}$$
$$i = H, K, U, L, B \quad (10.7)$$

The error terms, ϵ_{it}, are assumed to have zero means and constant variances. The use of ordinary least squares (OLS) to estimate (10.7) will result in biased estimates if the error terms are serially dependent. In order to test for first-order serial correlation, the demand equations are estimated by both OLS and a Cochrane-Orcutt procedure.

The OLS and Cochrane-Orcutt results are compared using the F-statistic discussed in Chapter 9. The null hypothesis that the first-order serial correlation coefficient is equal to zero is rejected at the 10 percent level for four of the five demand equations. Therefore, the results obtained using the Cochrane-Orcutt procedure are reported here.

The estimated parameters in the equation using shipments plus changes in inventories as the measure of output are very similar to those obtained using only shipments. Since the estimated standard errors are somewhat smaller when shipments are used, the results reported here are for this specification. Inclusion of a time variable to allow for trends in equilibrium output has little effect on the estimated parameters but does cause problems of collinearity. Therefore, the results reported here are for the equations excluding time.

Estimated parameters are shown in Table 10-2 together with their estimated standard errors. The short-run elasticities with respect to output are significant at the 5 percent level in all equations except the one for energy. The effect of output on input demand is largest for capacity utilization and next largest for labor stock. The insignificant effect of output on energy demand indicates that short-run forecasts of energy demand do not depend critically on predicted output.

Table 10–2
Estimates of Parameters of the Dynamic Model: Manufacturing[a]

Independent Variables	Dependent Variables				
	H	K	U	L	B
Constant	−4.699[b] (1.691)	−0.614 (1.734)	4.125 (3.171)	2.479 (2.889)	4.008[b] (0.901)
Q_t	0.095 (0.086)	0.142[b] (0.053)	1.001[b] (0.097)	0.619[b] (0.089)	0.174[b] (0.028)
P_H/P_B	−0.279[b] (0.124)	−0.100 (0.108)	0.162 (0.188)	0.015 (0.168)	0.038 (0.057)
P_K/P_B	−0.098[b] (0.043)	−0.046 (0.032)	0.116[b] (0.053)	0.117[b] (0.048)	0.032[b] (0.016)
H_{t-1}	0.175[b] (0.101)	0.094 (0.062)	−0.233[b] (0.105)	−0.152 (0.096)	−0.027 (0.033)
K_{t-1}	0.547[b] (0.113)	0.531[b] (0.105)	−0.245 (0.182)	−0.009 (0.158)	−0.034 (0.054)
U_{t-1}	−0.038 (0.130)	0.163 (0.145)	0.675[b] (0.286)	0.178 (0.260)	0.038 (0.074)
L_{t-1}	−0.204 (0.186)	0.342[b] (0.158)	−0.817[b] (0.265)	−0.152 (0.242)	−0.198[b] (0.083)
B_{t-1}	1.634[b] (0.490)	−1.195[b] (0.389)	−0.756 (0.779)	0.796 (0.708)	0.014 (0.197)
$\bar{R}^2$	0.998	0.990	0.905	0.836	0.818

[a]Figures in parentheses are estimated standard errors.
[b]Significant at the .05 level.

The relative price of capital is significant at the 5 percent level in four equations and at the 10 percent level in one more. However, the relative price of energy is significant only in the energy equation. The coefficients of the relative prices of capital and energy are equal to the estimated short-run elasticities with respect to these prices. The short-run elasticity with respect to the wage rate is equal to the negative of the sum of the capital and energy price elasticities. The elasticity with respect to the wage rate is significant only in the energy equation.

The estimated coefficients of the lagged endogenous variables are equal to the estimated elements of the matrix $(I - \Gamma)$. The elements of the matrix Γ are shown in Table 10–3. All own-adjustment coefficients are positive as required. The own-adjustment coefficient for labor stock is greater than unity but not significantly so.[6]

The own-adjustment coefficient for labor stock is largest, followed by the coefficients for average hours and energy. The magnitudes of these own-adjustment coefficients indicate that the corresponding inputs are truly variable.

Table 10-3
Adjustment Coefficients: Manufacturing

Independent Variables	Dependent Variables				
	H	K	U	L	B
H_{t-1}	0.825[a]	−0.094	0.233[b]	0.152	0.027
K_{t-1}	−0.547[b]	0.469[a]	0.245	0.009	0.034
U_{t-1}	0.038	−0.163	0.325[a]	−0.178	−0.038
L_{t-1}	0.204	−0.342[b]	0.817[b]	1.152	0.198[b]
B_{t-1}	−1.634[b]	1.195[b]	0.756	−0.796	0.986

[a]Significantly different from 1.0 at the .05 level.
[b]Significant at the .05 level.

The own-adjustment coefficient for capital stock is considerably smaller, as would be expected. The own-adjustment coefficient for utilization is smallest of all. This apparently incongruous result may be due to the use of capacity utilization rather than capital utilization for this variable.

Of the 20 cross-adjustment coefficients, 7 are significant at the 5 percent level. The coefficients of capital stock and average hours worked are both highly significant in the energy equation, indicating that excess demand for these inputs has a significant effect on energy demand. The coefficient of energy is significant only in the capacity utilization equation.

The matrix of cross-adjustment coefficients should be symmetric in signs. The estimated matrix satisfies this condition for only 4 of the 10 pairs of inputs. The failure of the model to satisfy the symmetry condition may be more apparent than real, since no nonsymmetric cases exist in which both of the coefficients are statistically significant. However, this is also true of the pairs of coefficients with the same sign.

Pairs of inputs for which the estimated cross-adjustment coefficients have the same sign are energy and capital, energy and capacity utilization, energy and labor stock, and capital stock and labor utilization. Energy and capital stock appear to be dynamic complements, while the other three pairs of inputs appear to be dynamic substitutes. Thus, excess demand for energy appears to increase labor stock and capacity utilization and decrease capital stock. These results provide information on the important policy question of the effect of temporary energy shortages on demand for other inputs, but must be considered highly tentative given the general lack of statistical significance of the estimated cross-adjustment coefficients.

All three short-run price elasticities for energy are significant at the .025 level. The time path of the price elasticities is shown in Table 10-4. The elasticities through year zero are equal to the estimated short-run elasticities. The

Table 10-4
Time Path of Energy Price Elasticities: Manufacturing

Inde-pendent Variable	Cumulative Elasticity Through Year						Long-Run Elasticity
	0	1	2	3	4	5	
P_H	−0.279	−0.330	−0.393	−0.437	−0.444	−0.437	−0.415
P_B	0.337	0.406	0.514	0.566	0.563	0.550	0.568
P_K	−0.098	−0.116	−0.162	−0.170	−0.160	−0.155	−0.153

estimated short-run own-price elasticity of demand for energy is −0.28, and the estimated short-run cross-elasticities of demand with respect to the hourly wage rate and the user cost of capital are 0.34 and −0.10 respectively.

The last column of Table 10-4 shows the estimated long-run price elasticities. The results indicate that energy and labor are substitutes and energy and capital are complements in the long run. The estimated long-run own-price elasticity of demand for energy is −0.42, and the estimated long-run cross-elasticities of demand with respect to the hourly wage rate and the user cost of capital are 0.57 and −0.15 respectively.

The estimated intermediate-run elasticities shown in Table 10-4 indicate quite rapid response to price changes. The cumulative elasticities through year three are approximately equal to the long-run elasticities. Two of the elasticities are actually slightly larger in absolute value than the long-run elasticities, indicating a small degree of overshooting in the intermediate-run response to price changes.

Dynamic stability of the system of demand equations is checked by calculating the characteristic roots of $(I - \Gamma)$. The characteristic roots for the matrix used in calculating the elasticities shown in Table 10-4 are $1.0019 \pm 0.0435i$, $0.0425 \pm 0.0275i$, and 0.0652. The condition that all characteristic roots be less than unity is not satisfied. However, the departure from the conditions for stability is small and its statistical significance cannot be determined. The existence of complex roots is consistent with the nonmonotonic behavior of the intermediate-run elasticities shown in Table 10-4.

Concluding Comments

The use of a dynamic model of demand for inputs provides new information on the characteristics of energy demand in U.S. manufacturing. The estimated cross-adjustment coefficients provide tentative evidence that energy is a dynamic complement of capital stock and a dynamic substitute for both labor stock and capacity utilization. Estimated short-run price elasticities of demand for energy are found to be statistically significant. The response of demand to price changes is quite rapid, with the full long-run response being approximately realized within three years after the year in which a price change occurs.

The estimated long-run price elasticities are similar to estimated elasticities reported in studies using static demand models. Berndt and Wood's (1975) study of U.S. manufacturing and Fuss' (1977) study of Canadian manufacturing also find that energy and capital are complements and that energy and labor are substitutes in the long run. The estimated long-run own-price elasticity of −0.42 in the present study is comparable to the value of −0.47 obtained by Berndt and Wood for 1959, the midyear of the sample period used here.[7] Thus it appears that the estimated elasticities of demand obtained with static models should be interpreted as long-run rather than short-run elasticities.

Notes

1. Griffin and Gregory (1976) discuss the relationship between cross-section and time-series results for static models and compare estimates obtained with international cross-section data to time-series results in Berndt and Wood (1975) and Hudson and Jorgenson (1974).

2. In practice, data on stocks of inputs are often used as proxies for services of inputs under the assumption that utilization rates are constant.

3. The Cobb-Douglas form can be interpreted as a translog form that is subject to the restrictions $\gamma_{ij} = 0$ for all i and j. Tests of these restrictions are discussed in Chapter 8.

4. If a translog cost function were used, a comparable adjustment function could be obtained by replacing the input variables in equation (10.4) by the corresponding cost shares.

5. The constraint that the firm is on its production function also implies singularity of $(I - \Gamma)$; see Nadiri and Rosen (1973, pp. 32–33). The restrictions are not imposed on the system of equations.

6. In calculating intermediate- and long-run elasticities, the value of the labor own-adjustment coefficient is set equal to one.

7. Fuss (1977) reports as a representative result for Canada an estimate of −0.49 at the means of the data for Ontario.

References

Acton, Jan, Bridger Mitchell, and Ragnhild Mowill. 1976. "Residential Demand for Electricity in Los Angeles: An Econometric Study of Disaggregated Data." Report R-1899-NSF, Santa Monica, Calif.: Rand Corporation.

Allen, R.G.D. 1966. *Mathematical Analysis For Economists*. New York: St. Martin's Press.

American Gas Association. Various Years. *Gas Facts*. Arlington, Virginia: American Gas Association.

Atkinson, Scott E., and Robert Halvorsen. 1976*a*. "Interfuel Substitution in Steam Electric Power Generation." *Journal of Political Economy* 84, no. 5: 959-78.

_____. 1976*b*. "Demand for Fossil Fuels by Electric Utilities." In *Econometric Dimensions of Energy Demand and Supply*, ed. A. Bradley Askin and John Kraft. Lexington, Mass.: D.C. Heath and Co., Lexington Books.

_____. 1977. "A Test of Relative and Absolute Price Efficiency in Regulated Utilities." Discussion Paper No. 77-7. Seattle, Wash.: Institute for Economic Research, University of Washington.

Averch, Harvey, and Leland L. Johnson. 1962. "Behavior of the Firm Under Regulatory Constraint." *American Economic Review* 52, no. 5: 1052-69.

Bailey, Elizabeth E. 1973. *Economic Theory of Regulatory Constraint*. Lexington, Mass.: D.C. Heath and Co., Lexington Books.

Barzel, Yoram. 1963. "Productivity in the Electric Power Industry, 1929-1955." *Review of Economics and Statistics* 45, no. 4: 395-408.

_____. 1964. "The Production Function and Technical Change in the Steam-Power Industry." *Journal of Political Economy* 72, no. 2: 133-50.

Baumol, William J., and Alvin K. Klevorick. 1970. "Input Choices and Rate of Return Regulation: An Overview of the Discussion." *The Bell Journal of Economics and Management Science* 1: no. 2: 169-90.

Belinfante, Alexander E. 1969. "Technical Change in the Steam Electric Power Generating Industry." Ph.D. dissertation, University of California, Berkeley.

Berndt, Ernst R. 1977. "Notes on Generalized R^2." Mimeographed. Vancouver, B.C.: University of British Columbia.

Berndt, Ernst R. and Dale W. Jorgenson. 1973. "Production Structure." In *U.S. Energy Resources and Economic Growth, Final Report to the Ford Foundation Energy Policy Project*. Cambridge, Mass.

Berndt, Ernst R., and Eugene N. Savin. 1977. "Conflict Among Criteria for Testing Hypotheses in the Multivariate Linear Regression Model." *Econometrica* 45, no. 5: 1263-77.

Berndt, Ernst R., and David O. Wood. 1975. "Technology, Prices and the Derived Demand for Energy." *Review of Economics and Statistics* 57, no. 3: 259-268.

Binswanger, Hans P. 1974. "The Measurement of Technical Change Biases With Many Factors of Production." *American Economic Review* 64, no. 6: 964-76.

Brown's Directory of North American Gas Companies. Various Years. New York: Moore.

Burgess, David F. 1974. "Production Theory and the Derived Demand for Imports." *Journal of International Economics* 4, no. 2: 103-17.

Chern, Wen S. 1976. "Industrial Demand for Energy." Mimeographed. Oak Ridge, Tenn.: Oak Ridge National Laboratory.

Christensen, Laurits R. 1973. "Simultaneous Statistical Inference in the Normal Multiple Linear Regression Model." *Journal of the American Statistical Association* 68, no. 342: 457-61.

Christensen, Laurits R., and William H. Greene. 1976. "Economies of Scale in U.S. Electric Power Generation." *Journal of Political Economy* 84, no. 4: 655-676.

Christensen, Laurits R., and Marilyn E. Manser. 1977. "Estimating U.S. Consumer Preferences for Meat with a Flexible Utility Function." *Journal of Econometrics* 5, no. 1: 37-53.

Christensen, Laurits R., Dale W. Jorgenson, and Lawrence J. Lau. 1971. "Conjugate Duality and the Transcendental Logarithmic Production Function." *Econometrica* 39, no. 4: 255-56.

_____. 1973. "Transcendental Logarithmic Production Frontiers." *Review of Economics and Statistics* 55, no. 1: 28-45.

Cochrane, D., and G.H. Orcutt. 1949. "Application of Least Squares Regressions to Relationships Containing Autocorrelated Error Terms." *Journal of the American Statistical Association* 44: 32-61.

Courville, Leon. 1974. "Regulation and Efficiency in the Electric Utility Industry." *The Bell Journal of Economics and Management Science* 5, no. 1: 53-74.

Cowing, Thomas G. 1970. "Technical Change in Steam-Electric Generation: An Engineering Approach." Ph.D. dissertation, University of California, Berkeley.

Dhrymes, Phoebus J., and Mordecai Kurz. 1964. "Technology and Scale in Electricity Generation." *Econometrica* 32, no. 3: 287-315.

Diamond, P.A., and D.L. McFadden. 1974. "Some Uses of the Expenditure Function in Public Finance." *Journal of Public Economics* 3, no. 1: 3-21.

Diewert, W.E. 1971. "An Application of the Shepard Duality Theorem: A Generalized Leontief Production Function." *Journal of Political Economy* 79, no. 3: 481-507.

_____. 1973. "Separability and a Generalization of the Cobb-Douglas Cost, Production and Indirect Utility Functions." Mimeographed. Vancouver, B.C.: Department of Economics, University of British Columbia.

_____. 1974. "Applications of Duality Theory." In *Frontiers in Quantitative Economics*, vol. 2, ed. M. Intriligator and D. Kendrick. Amsterdam: North-Holland.

_____. 1976. "Exact and Superlative Index Numbers." *Journal of Econometrics* 4, no. 2: 115-45.

Edison Electric Institute. Various Years. *Statistical Year Book of the Electric Utility Industry*. New York: Edison Electric Institute.

Fisher, Franklin M., and Carl Kaysen. 1962. *A Study in Econometrics: The Demand for Electricity in the United States*. Amsterdam: North-Holland.

Fuss, Melvyn A. 1970. "The Time Structure of Technology: An Empirical Analysis of the Putty-Clay Hypothesis." Ph.D. dissertation, University of California, Berkeley.

_____. 1971. "Factor Substitution in Electricity Generation: A Test of the Putty-Clay Hypothesis." Discussion paper no. 185. Cambridge, Mass.: Harvard Institute of Economic Research, Harvard University.

_____. 1977. "The Demand for Energy in Canadian Manufacturing: An Example of the Estimation of Production Structures with Many Inputs." *Journal of Econometrics* 5, no. 1: 89-116.

Galatin, Malcolm. 1968. *Economies of Scale and Technological Change in Thermal Power Generation*. Amsterdam: North-Holland.

Goldberger, Arthur S. 1964. *Econometric Theory*. New York: Wiley.

Goldfeld, Stephen M., and Richard E. Quandt. 1965. "Some Tests for Homoscedasticity." *Journal of the American Statistical Association* 60: 539-547.

Griffin, James M., and Paul R. Gregory. 1976. "An Intercountry Translog Model of Energy Substitution Responses." *American Economic Review* 66, no. 5: 845-57.

Griliches, Zvi. 1967. "Distributed Lags: A Survey." *Econometrica* 35, no. 1: 16-49.

Halvorsen, Robert. 1972. "Residential Demand for Electricity." Ph.D. dissertation, Harvard University.

_____. 1975. "Residential Demand for Electric Energy." *Review of Economics and Statistics* 57, no. 1: 12-18.

_____. 1976. "Demand for Electric Energy in the United States." *Southern Economic Journal* 42, no. 4: 610-25.

_____. 1977. "Energy Substitution in U.S. Manufacturing." *Review of Economics and Statistics* 59, no. 4: 381-88.

Halvorsen, Robert, and Jay Ford. 1978. "Substitution Among Energy, Capital, and Labor Inputs in U.S. Manufacturing." In *Advances in the Economics of Energy and Resources: Vol. I. The Structure of Energy Markets*, ed. Robert S. Pindyck. Greenwich, Conn.: JAI Press.

Houthakker, H.S., and Lester D. Taylor. 1966. *Consumer Demand in the United States, 1929-1970*. Cambridge, Mass.: Harvard University Press.

Hudson, Edward A., and Dale W. Jorgenson. 1974. "U.S. Energy Policy and Economic Growth, 1975–2000." *Bell Journal of Economics and Management Science* 5, no. 2: 461–514.

Iulo, William. 1961. *Electrical Utilities–Costs and Performance.* Pullman: Washington State University Press.

Johnston, J. 1972. *Econometric Methods.* 2d ed. New York: McGraw-Hill.

Jorgenson, Dale W., and Lawrence J. Lau. 1975. "The Structure of Consumer Preferences." *Annals of Economic and Social Measurement* 4, no. 1: 49–101.

Joskow, Paul L., and Frederic S. Mishkin. 1974. "Electric Utility Fuel Choice in the United States." Mimeographed. Cambridge, Mass.: Massachusetts Institute of Technology.

Kmenta, Jan. 1971. *Elements of Econometrics.* New York: Macmillan.

Komiya, Ryutaro. 1962. "Technological Progress and the Production Function in the United States Steam Power Industry." *Review of Economics and Statistics* 44, no. 2: 156–66.

Koyck, L.M. 1954. *Distributed Lags and Investment Analysis.* Amsterdam: North-Holland.

Kuh, Edwin. 1963. *Capital Stock Growth.* Amsterdam: North-Holland.

Lau, Lawrence J. 1969. "Some Applications of Profit Functions." Memorandum No. 86A and B. Stanford, Calif.: Research Center in Economic Growth, Stanford University.

———. 1974a. "A Characterization of the Normalized Restricted Profit Function." Technical report no. 134. Stanford, Calif.: Institute for Mathematical Studies in the Social Sciences, Stanford University.

———. 1974b. "Applications of Duality Theory: A Comment." In *Frontiers in Quantitative Economics*, vol. 2, ed. M. Intriligator and D. Kendrick. Amsterdam: North-Holland.

———. 1974c. "Econometrics of Monotonicity, Convexity and Quasiconvexity." Technical report no. 123. Stanford, Calif.: Institute for Mathematical Studies in the Social Sciences, Stanford University.

———. 1974d. "Homothetic Production Functions." Unpublished memorandum. Stanford University.

Lau, Lawrence J., and Pan A. Yotopoulos. 1971. "A Test for Relative Efficiency and Application to Indian Agriculture." *American Economic Review* 61, no. 1: 94–109.

Lawrence, Anthony G. 1972. "Inter-fuel Substitution: Steam Electric Generation's Demand for Fuels." Research discussion paper no. 8. Washington: Research Division, Office of Prices and Living Conditions, U.S. Bureau of Labor Statistics.

Ling, Suilin. 1964. *Economies of Scale in the Steam-Electric Power Generating Industry: An Analytical Approach.* Amsterdam: North-Holland.

Lomax, K.S. 1952. "Cost Curves for Electricity Generation." *Economica* 19, no. 74: 193–97.

McFadden, Daniel. 1964. "Notes on the Estimation of the Elasticity of Substitution." Working paper no. 57. Berkeley, Calif.: Institute of Business and Economic Research, University of California, Berkeley.

Meyer, Robert A. 1976. "Optimal Nonlinear Pricing Structures: An Application to Energy Pricing." Mimeographed. Berkeley, Calif.: University of California.

Mount, T.D., L.D. Chapman, and T.J. Tyrell. 1973. "Electricity Demand in the United States: An Econometric Analysis." Report ORNL-NSF-EP-4P. Oak Ridge, Tenn.: Oak Ridge National Laboratory.

Nadiri, M. Ishaq, and Sherwin Rosen. 1969. "Interrelated Factor Demand Functions." *American Economic Review* 59, no. 4: 457-71.

_____. 1973. *A Disequilibrium Model of Demand for Factors of Production.* New York: National Bureau of Economic Research.

Nerlove, Marc. 1963. "Returns to Scale in Electricity Supply." In *Measurement in Economics: Studies in Mathematical Economics and Econometrics in Memory of Yehuda Grunfeld,* ed. Carl F. Christ. Stanford, Calif.: Stanford University Press.

Nordin, J.A. 1947. "Note on a Light Plant's Cost Curves." *Econometrica* 40, no. 3: 231-35.

Oberhofer, W., and J. Kmenta. 1974. "A General Procedure for Obtaining Maximum Likelihood Estimates in Generalized Regression Models." *Econometrica* 42, no. 3: 579-90.

Parks, Richard W. 1971. "Price Responsiveness of Factor Utilization in Swedish Manufacturing, 1870-1950." *Review of Economics and Statistics* 53, no. 2: 129-39.

Spann, Robert M. 1974. "Rate of Return Regulation and Efficiency in Production: An Empirical Test of the Averch-Johnson Thesis." *Bell Journal of Economics and Management Science* 5, no. 1: 38-52.

Taylor, Lester D. 1975. "The Demand for Electricity: A Survey." *Bell Journal of Economics* 6, no. 1: 74-110.

Theil, Henri. 1957. "Specification Errors and the Estimation of Economic Relationships." *Review of the International Statistical Institute* 25: 41-51.

U.S. Bureau of the Census. 1969. *Annual Survey of Manufacturing.* Washington: Government Printing Office.

_____. 1960, 1970. *Census of Housing.* Washington: Government Printing Office.

_____. 1958, 1962, 1972. *Census of Manufactures.* Washington: Government Printing Office.

_____. 1962. *County and City Data Book.* Washington: Government Printing Office.

_____. 1976. *Manufacturer's Shipments, Inventories and Orders.* Washington: Government Printing Office.

_____. Various Years. *Statistical Abstract*. Washington: Government Printing Office.

U.S. Bureau of Labor Statistics. Various Years. *Wholesale Prices and Price Indexes*. Washington: Government Printing Office.

U.S. Department of Commerce. Various Years. *Survey of Current Business*. Washington: Government Printing Office.

U.S. Department of Labor. 1976. *The Employment Situation*. Washington: Government Printing Office.

U.S. Federal Power Commission. Undated. "Instructions for Reporting Typical Net Monthly Bills for Electric Service." Washington: Government Printing Office.

_____. 1973a. *Statistics of Privately Owned Electric Utilities in the United States: 1972*. Washington: Government Printing Office.

_____. 1973b. *Steam-Electric Plant Air and Water Quality Control Data for the Year Ending December 31, 1970*. Washington: Government Printing Office.

_____. 1974. *Steam-Electric Plant Construction Cost and Annual Production Expenses: Twenty-Fifth Annual Supplement–1972*. Washington: Government Printing Office.

_____. Various Years. *Typical Electric Bills*. Washington: Government Printing Office.

Wharton Econometric Forecasting Associates. 1976. "Wharton Econometric Forecasting Associates Release." Philadelphia, Penn.

Yotopolous, Pan A., and Lawrence J. Lau. 1973. "A Test for Relative Efficiency: Some Further Results." *American Economic Review* 63, no. 1: 214–23.

Zellner, Arnold. 1962. "An Efficient Method of Estimating Seemingly Unrelated Regressions and Tests for Aggregation Bias." *Journal of the American Statistical Association* 57, no. 298: 348–68.

Index

Acton, Jan, 8n

Adaptive-expectations models, 138, 139

Adding-up restrictions, 78, 80, 100

Adjustment function, dynamic manufacturing model, 154

Allen, R.G.D., 74n

Allen partial elasticities of substitution. *See* Elasticities of substitution

American Gas Association, 23, 60

Analyses of covariance: disaggregation by level of price, 33; pooling of cross-section data, 13, 19, 27, 29, 37, 41, 47, 54; regional demand equations, 32

Atkinson, Scott E., 69n, 71n, 95n

Average electricity prices, 1, 7, 10, 101n, 135; use of, in place of marginal price, 10–11, 15–16

Averch, Harvey, 71n, 85n

Averch-Johnson effect, 71

Bailey, Elizabeth E., 71n, 85n

Barzel, Yoram, 71n, 85n

Baumol, William J., 71n

Belinfante, Alexander E., 85n

Berndt, Ernst R., 69n, 76n, 99n, 104, 120, 151, 151n, 156, 160

Beta coefficients, 26–27, 40

Binswanger, Hans P., 69n

Bonferroni t-tests, 93n

Brown's Directory of North American Gas Companies, 53

Burgess, David F., 69n

CES functional form, 69, 85

Chapman, L.D., 99n, 151

Chern, Wen S., 151

Choice of price variable, 1, 7–8

Christensen, Laurits R., 69n, 71n, 85n, 93n

Coal: consumption of, by electric utilities, 69, 85; share of, in manufacturing energy purchases, 76, 99

Cobb-Douglas functional form, 69, 77, 152; tests of, 3, 122–123

Cochrane, D., 140

Cochrane-Orcutt procedure, 140–142, 147, 156

Commercial and industrial electricity demand, 2, 55–64

Concavity of cost function, 80–81, 103–104

Convexity of profit function, 72–73, 88

Cost function, 2–3, 69, 76–82, 99–105, 121–124

Courville, Leon, 71n

Cowing, Thomas G., 85n

Cross-equation equality restrictions. *See* Equality restrictions

Data sources: commercial and industrial electricity demand, 60; dynamic energy demand in manufacturing, 155–156; energy substitution in manufacturing, 99, 101; interfuel substitution in electric power, 87; long-run residential electricity demand, 23–24, 39, 47n, 52–53; short-run residential electricity demand, 140–141

Dependence of price on quantity purchased, 1, 7–9, 16, 37

Dhrymes, Phoebus J., 71n, 85n

Diamond, Peter A., 69n

Diewert, W.E., 69, 69n, 72, 77, 79n

Direct elasticities of demand, definition of, 9

Disaggregation: by geographic area. *See* Regional equations; by level of price, 1, 19, 32–34

Duality theory, 2, 69; and cost function, 77, 99; and profit function, 70, 72, 85–86

Dynamic complements and substitutes, 151, 155, 158–159

Dynamic cross-section equations, 13–15, 16; demand, 19, 29, 32; price, 41, 45; reduced-form, 48, 54

Dynamic energy demand in manufacturing, 3, 151–160

Dynamic specification of time-series equations, 137–139; tests of, 142, 147–148

Dynamic stability, 155, 159

Edison Electric Institute, 23, 39, 60, 140

Elasticities of demand. *See* Electricity demand elasticities; Energy demand elasticities in manufacturing; Fuel demand elasticities in electric power generation

Elasticities of substitution: a priori restrictions on, 69, 72; energy substitution in manufacturing, 81, 118; interfuel substitution in electric power generation, 74, 91–93; interpretation of, as normalized price elasticities, 81

Elasticity of expenditure on electricity, 49

Elasticity of price with respect to quantity purchased, 49

Elasticity of unit cost of energy with respect to energy prices, 104

Electricity demand elasticities: commercial, 2, 55, 61–62; industrial 2, 55, 59–60, 62–64; long-run residential: direct, 1, 7, 9–10, 16, 19, 25, 34–35; total, 1–2, 7, 9, 10–11, 16, 37, 45–49, 51, 53–54; short-run residential, 139–140; for nation, 3, 135, 148; for states, 3, 135, 141–142

Electricity demand models. *See* Commercial and industrial electricity demand; Long-run residential electricity demand; Short-run residential electricity demand

Electricity price schedule. *See* Dependence of price on quantity purchased

Electricity, share of, in manufacturing energy purchases, 76, 99

Energy demand elasticities in manufacturing: aggregate energy input, 3, 82, 120, 154–155, 158–160; individual energy inputs; for total manufacturing, 3, 100, 118, 120–121, 124; for two-digit industries, 3, 81–82, 99–100, 105, 118, 120–121

Energy-input aggregator function, 76–77, 122–123

Energy intensiveness of production, 99

Energy substitution in manufacturing, 2–3, 76–82, 99–124

Equality restrictions: for cost function, 78–79, 80, 102; for profit function, 72, 88, 93

Estimation procedures: commercial and industrial electricity demand, 55, 60; dynamic energy demand in manufacturing, 156; energy substitution in manufacturing, 100–101; interfuel substitution in electric power, 86–87; long-run residential electricity demand, 9–12, 24, 39–40, 47; short-run residential electricity demand, 139–141

Euler's theorem, 78

Fisher, Franklin M., 99n

Flexible functional forms, 69, 71–72

Ford, Jay, 69n, 86n

F-statistics, 13, 121–122, 140, 142

Fuel demand elasticities in electric power generation, 73, 90–93

Fuel oil: consumption of, by electric utilities, 69, 85; share of, in manufacturing energy purchases, 99

Fuss, Melvyn A., 69n, 71n, 85n, 99n, 160, 160n

Galatin, Malcolm, 85n
Gas: consumption of, by electric utilities, 69, 85; share of, in manufacturing energy purchases, 76, 99
Geometrically declining lag structure, 15, 137–138, 139, 141
Goldberger, Arthur S., 26
Goldfeld, Stephen M., 24
Goodness of fit: profit function, 88; reduced-form equation, 47, 53; system of cost share equations, 104
Greene, William H., 69n, 85n
Gregory, Paul R., 99n, 151n
Griffin, James M., 99n, 151n
Griliches, Zvi, 14n
Groupwise homogeneity, 75
Groupwise homotheticity, 75, 93

Habit-formation models, 138–139
Halvorsen, Robert, 9n, 25n, 40n, 69n, 71n, 76n, 95n
Hessian: of cost function, 80; of profit function, 73, 88
Heteroscedasticity, 24
Hicksian neutrality, 75, 94
Homogeneity, tests of, using profit function, 2, 74–75, 86, 93, 95. *See also* Linear homogeneity
Homotheticity, tests of, using profit function, 74, 93
Hotelling's lemma, 71, 73
Houthakker, Hendrik S., 138n
Hudson, Edward A., 151, 151n

Identification of electricity demand equation, 1, 7–8
Income elasticity of expenditure on electricity, 49
Interfuel substitution in electric power generation, 2, 69–76, 85–95
Inverted rate schedules, 10n
Inverted-V lag structure, 14–15

Iterative Zellner-efficient estimation, 72, 80, 87, 101n
Iulo, William, 85n

Johnson, Leland L., 71n
Johnston, J., 138
Jorgenson, Dale W., 69n, 71n, 80n, 99n, 103n, 151, 151n
Joskow, Paul L., 85, 85n

Kaysen, Carl, 99n
Klevorick, Alvin K., 71n
Kmenta, Jan, 72n, 105
Komiya, Ryutaro, 85n
Koyck, L.M., 137
Koyck transformation, 137–139
Kuh, Edwin, 13
Kurz, Mordecai, 71n, 85n

Lag structures, cross-section equations, 13–15
Lau, Lawrence J., 69, 69n, 71, 71n, 72, 74, 75, 77, 80n, 103n
Lawrence, Anthony G., 85, 85n
Level of price, effect on own-price elasticity of, 1, 19, 32–34
Likelihood ratio tests, 76, 102, 123
Linear homogeneity: of cost function, 78, 80, 81; of energy-input function, 77, 82
Ling, Suilin, 85n
Log-linear functional form, 1, 9, 15, 25, 34, 40, 53, 137, 154–155
Lomax, K.S., 85n
Long-run residential electricity demand, 1–2, 7–16, 19–35, 37–49, 51–54

McFadden, Daniel L., 69n, 85n
Manser, Marilyn E., 69n
Marginal electricity price, 1, 7–10, 15
Measurement errors, 11, 20–21, 26, 47, 51–53
Meyer, Robert A., 8n
Mishkin, Frederic S., 85, 85n
Mitchell, Bridger, 8n

Model specification: commercial and industrial electricity demand, 55–60; dynamic energy demand in manufacturing, 151–155; energy substitution in manufacturing, 76–82, 100–101; interfuel substitution in electric power, 69–76, 86; long-run residential electricity demand, 7–9, 19–23; short-run residential electricity demand, 135–139

Monotonicity: of cost function, 80, 103; of profit function, 72–73, 88

Mount, T.D., 99n, 151

Mowill, Ragnhild, 8n

Multicollinearity, 8, 11–12, 137

Nadiri, M. Ishaq, 151, 155, 155n

National Bureau of Economic Research, 76n

Nerlove, Marc, 85n, 93n

Nordin, J.A., 85n

Normalized restricted profit function, 2, 69–76, 77n, 82n, 85–89

Oberhofer, W., 72n

Orcutt, G.H., 140

Ordinary least squares, 11, 47, 61n, 86, 140–142, 147, 156

Parameter estimates: commercial and industrial electricity demand, 60–64; dynamic energy demand in manufacturing, 156–157; energy substitution in manufacturing, 104–105; interfuel substitution in electric power, 88; long-run residential electricity demand, 25–27, 29, 32–34, 37, 40–41, 45, 47–48, 53–54; short-run residential electricity demand, 141–142

Parks, Richard W., 69n

Partial-adjustment model, 138–139

Pascal distribution, 15

Performance of model: energy substitution in manufacturing, 2–3, 99, 101–104, 124; interfuel substitution in electric power, 2, 88–89, 95

Pooling of cross-section data, 13–14, 19, 27, 29, 37, 41, 47, 54

Production function: electric power generation, 70; manufacturing, 76, 151–152

Profit function. *See* Normalized restricted profit function

Pseudo-R^2, 104

Putty-clay technology, 85–86

Quandt, Richard E., 24

Reduced-form equation, 1–3, 9, 11–12, 16, 37, 45–48, 51–54, 135, 139–140

Regional equations: electricity demand, 1, 19, 32; electricity price, 37, 45

Regulatory lags, 12, 135

Response path of input demand to price change, 3, 155

Returns to scale in electric power generation, 2, 75, 85–86, 93, 95

Robustness of results. *See* Dynamic cross-section equations

Rosen, Sherwin, 151, 155, 155n

Savin, Eugene N., 76n

Separability: energy-input function, 80, 103; production function, 76

Serial correlation, 140–141, 156

Share elasticities, 104–105

Shepard's lemma, 77, 81

Short-run residential electricity demand, 3, 13, 135–149

Spann, Robert M., 71n

Specification errors, 21–22, 53

Specification of equations. *See* Model specification

Speed of response to price change, aggregate manufacturing, 3, 151, 159–160

Standard errors of elasticities at means of data, 105

Symmetry conditions, 72

Taxation of electricity, distributional effects of, 49

Taylor, Lester D., 8n, 138n

Technological change: electric power generation, 2, 71, 75, 86, 94, 95; manufacturing energy-input function, 3, 121–122

Tests of hypotheses: *See* Analyses of covariance; Cobb-Douglas functional form, tests of; Dynamic specification, tests of; Equality restrictions; Groupwise homogeneity; Groupwise homotheticity; Homogeneity; Homotheticity; Monotonicity; Serial correlation; Separability; Technological change

Theil, Henri, 21

Total elasticities of demand, definition of, 9

Total income elasticity of expenditure on electricity, 49

Translog functional form: for profit function, 71, 72; for cost function, 77, 152

Two-digit industries: energy consumption by, 99; production function for, 76

Two-stage least squares, 10, 24, 39

Typical electric bill data, 1, 11; use of, to estimate price equations, 55, 60; use of, to estimate reduced-form equations, 11–12, 16, 47–48, 135–136, 140

Tyrell, T.J., 99n, 151

Unit cost function. *See* Cost function

U.S. Bureau of the Census, 24, 39, 52, 53, 60, 156

U.S. Bureau of Labor Statistics, 23, 156

U.S. Department of Commerce, 23, 24, 39, 52, 60, 140–141

U.S. Department of Labor, 156

U.S. Federal Power Commission, 1, 11, 47n, 52, 60, 87, 140

Utilization rates of inputs, 152

Value added in manufacturing, 2, 59–60, 63

Wharton Econometric Forecasting Associates, 155

Wood, David O., 69n, 99n, 120, 151, 151n, 156, 160

Yotopoulos, Pan A., 69n

Zellner, Arnold, 72n

Zellner-efficient estimation. *See* Iterative Zellner-efficient estimation

About the Author

Robert Halvorsen is assistant professor of economics at the University of Washington. He received the B.B.A. from the University of Michigan and the M.B.A., M.P.A., and Ph.D. in economics from Harvard University. Dr. Halvorsen is the author of a number of articles on energy demand and he has served as a consultant for numerous agencies, including the Environmental Protection Agency, the Federal Energy Administration, and the Department of the Interior.